THE PORTABLE DAD

THE PORTABLE DAD

BY STEVE ELLIOTT

FIX-IT ADVICE FOR WHEN DAD'S NOT AROUND

9 8 7 6 5 4 3 2 1
Digit on the right indicates the number of this printing

Library of Congress Control Number: 2009920359

ISBN 978-0-7624-3528-9

Cover and interior design by Matthew Goodman
Cover illustrations by Carl Wiens
Interior illustrations by Harry Campbell
Edited by Kristen Green Wiewora
Typography: Archer and Chronicle

Running Press Book Publishers
2300 Chestnut Street
Philadelphia, PA 19103-4371

Visit us on the web!
www.runningpress.com

4

DEDICATION:
To Diane, Gina, and Frankie,
who give me reason to build.

TABLE OF CONTENTS

ACKNOWLEDGMENTS

When I was seven or eight, my grandpa gave me carpenter's tools for my birthday. They weren't toys, but real tools—a crosscut saw, hammer, square, coping saw, and tape measure. And he told me that with those tools he could build a house.

I never learned how to build houses, but I did learn how to use tools. More accurately, I had people who taught me. So Grandpa, Dad, Larry, Scott, and anyone else who ever bought, loaned or taught me how to use a tool or build anything, thank you. Without you, this book wouldn't have been possible.

I'd also like to thank Alison Picard, who recognized the potential of *The Portable Dad* before anyone else, and Running Press for embracing the concept. Like a talented general contractor, book editor Kristen Green Wiewora has been tireless in bringing this project to life. She's made the writing better and brought in other craftsmen—Carl Wiens and Harry Campbell, who did the outstanding illustrations, Mathew Goodman, who designed the inside pages, and Erin Slonaker, who did the copy editing and proofreading—to make the book you hold today a reality. Thank you all.

INTRODUCTION

This is not your typical "how-to" book.

Typical how-to books are written for super-handy people, or people who want to be super-handy, or people who like knowing how things work.

They are not written for folks like my daughter, Gina, who couldn't care less how things work so long as they work, and work right, and work right the first time. About three weeks after moving into her first apartment, she called home, stuck on her front porch.

"My key won't work," she said, quite annoyed.

"Are you at the right apartment?" I asked, annoying her quite a bit more.

Her reply was unprintable, and yes, she was at the right apartment. But the lock was gummed up, and it took some wiggling before the key finally slid in.

"The lock's just sticky," I told her. "Spray some WD-40 in it, and it'll be fine."

"What's WD-40?" she asked.

WD-40 is a spray lubricant that comes in a blue and yellow can, and until that moment I thought it was as ubiquitous and well-known as milk. I realized right then that there were some important things all those college-prep courses hadn't taught her, and I started writing this book.

The Portable Dad is the how-to book for people who don't really care to know, or who never had the opportunity to learn, how to. It doesn't give instructions for dozens of fun and exciting projects like other how-to books. It won't teach you how to rewire a lamp, install in-ground sprinklers, or restore a 1964 Chevy pickup. You won't be wielding weird contraptions by Chapter 9, and if you don't know what a torque wrench is now, you won't by the end of the book, either. (And quite honestly, you'll never need to know. Sleep easy.)

Instead, *The Portable Dad* just covers the basics—the stuff you need to know and need to do to take care of your car, bicycle, computer, and apartment. What this book will do is give you the basic information to keep your car alive and running—and safe. It'll help you keep your computer healthy and running and safe. It'll get you through the front door if the lock's gummed up, get a clogged drain to work, and even help get your deposit back despite the fact you put 623 holes in your bedroom walls when you weren't supposed to hang anything at all. It'll help you move out and move in, paint an apartment if you really want to, and take care of a lawn if you have to.

It'll help you with the stuff proud dads everywhere would love to show you and teach you and do for you if you just lived close enough.

CHAPTER 1:

CARS

The great news about cars today is that they are better built and safer than ever before. (If your grandpa or some other old-timer complains, "They don't make them like they used to . . ." the proper reply is, "Thank God and the Japanese.") Americans used to accept and even expect a certain degree of unreliability from their cars, until Japanese imports in the 1970s spoiled us all by working well pretty much all the time. Newer cars are even better, and with just a little effort on your part, will get you to and from school, Starbucks, and spring break for many years to come.

This chapter covers the few things you need to do to keep your car running well and on the road.

OIL

WHAT A DIPSTICK!

Nothing is more important to keeping your car alive than oil. Without oil, your Civic hatchback dies a quick and ugly death. Here's why: Inside your engine, a whole bunch of metal pieces are spinning and sliding against a whole bunch of other metal pieces, and they are doing it thousands of times a minute. Without oil, those metal parts rub directly on each other, metal on metal, and the heat and friction grinds your motor to bits in a matter of minutes.

Oil works by forming a sticky film between the moving metal parts so they don't actually rub against each other. Instead, they rub against a film of oil very *near* each other. It makes all the difference in the world. Drive your car without oil, and your engine becomes a heavy and expensive paperweight inside two miles. Keep the oil flowing and fresh, and as long as you don't drive off the Santa Monica Pier, you can be driving your car after 200,000 miles. So: check and change your oil regularly.

I know your dashboard has a little red light shaped like an oil lamp and that it'll light up if your car ever runs out of oil. The problem is, if that ever happens, bad things are already happening.

CHECK YOUR OIL

YOU'LL NEED: A PAPER TOWEL. YOU'LL NEED TO: PARK SOMEWHERE FLAT AND DO THIS WITH THE ENGINE OFF.

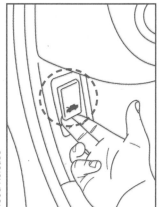

Hood Release

1. Open the hood. The hood release is somewhere under the dash to your left as you sit in the driver's seat. In many cars, the parking brake release is down there somewhere too, so if the lever you pull doesn't release the hood, keep looking.

When you pull the hood release lever, the hood will pop up maybe an inch or so. It won't open all the way, because it has a safety latch. The safety latch keeps the hood from flying open and blocking your view while you're driving down the freeway. (Blind driving is even worse than blind dating.)

2 . So step two is to release the safety latch. Stand in front of the car at the center and reach under the popped-up hood. The latch will pull, or push, or go to the side—different cars do it differently. Peek under or push around until your latch releases, then lift the hood.

Some cars have springs that hold the hood up. Some don't. If yours doesn't, it'll have a skinny metal bar that lifts up and props the hood open. The end of the bar will fit into a slot or hole on the hood to hold it securely. Find it and use it—dropping a car hood on your head or hands will ruin your whole day.

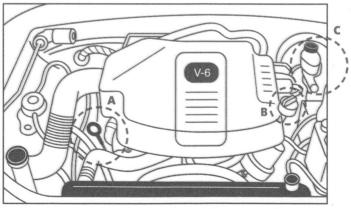

(A) Oil dipstick (B) Oil cap (C) Brake fluid reservoir

3 . Okay, hood's open. Engine is off. What you're looking for is the dipstick **(see figure A, page 13)**. (How "dipstick" became an insulting personal description is one of those Mysteries of the Universe.) It'll have a small handle, and if it's nice it'll be labeled "Oil." It might have that silly oil lamp icon on it. It might be labeled "Engine." It might have nothing. Look in the front area of the engine. (There is another dipstick, usually at the back of the engine, to check transmission fluid, but that's not the one we're looking for.) Found it? Good.

4 . Pull it out. What you'll find is a flat flexible piece of metal with markings—and a bit of oil—at the bottom end. Use your paper towel to wipe away that oil, then put the dipstick back where you found it. Push it all the way in, then pull it back out and hold it sideways to read the oil level.

5 . The marking closest to the end may be labeled "Low" or "Add." Maybe just "L." It could be just a dot or line stamped into the metal. If the top edge of the oil film that's sticking to your dipstick is below that mark, you'll need to add oil. (We'll get to how in a minute.) At the top end of the markings, there's a full mark. When you add oil, you want to bring it up to that mark but not go over.

6 . If your oil level is okay, the oil sticking to your dipstick will fall somewhere between the "add" and "full" marks. If so, you're perfect. Put the dipstick back, close the hood, throw away the paper towel, and you're good to go. If you're low, the dipstick will give you an idea of how low. A long way below the add mark means you'll need to put in a full quart or more—ouch! Just a little below the mark means a half-quart might do the trick. Either way, you're going to need some oil.

BUYING OIL

Oil comes in different weights and grades, and any big-box superstore like Wal Mart, K-mart, or Target will have at least a dozen different brands on the shelves. Auto stores have even more choices, and even your local grocery or gas station convenience store will have at least a few different options.

Your owner's manual will tell you what kind of oil to use. If you don't have it, you'll typically want 5W-30 or 10W-40 oil from any of the major brands: Castrol, Valvoline, Pennzoil, Chevron, Havoline, Quaker State, etc. There are others. If all you want to do is get your engine topped up with oil, pick any of the major brands off the shelf of any parts store or discount retailer and take it home. It'll work, and it'll be a dang sight better than driving a quart low. Pick 10W-40 if you live somewhere hot—where it gets to 95 degrees or higher in the summer. If it's cold where you live, 5W-30 will be fine. There are synthetic oils and synthetic blends, but unless your car needs one for some specific reason, you'll do just fine with regular ("conventional") motor oil. It'll cost you around $2 a quart.

Why is it called 5W-30 or 10W-40? That gets into the "weight" of oil, which has nothing to do with how much it actually weighs. The "weight" of an oil tells you how thick or thin it is. Smaller numbers mean thin oil. Bigger numbers are thicker oils. Thin oil gets into narrower spaces and gets there quicker, but it doesn't protect as well as thick oil. Thin oils are great when it's cold and you first start your car. But oil gets thinner as it heats up, and a thin oil will get too thin. A thick oil provides perfect protection once it heats up, but it doesn't cut it in the cold because it's too thick to flow into the tiny spaces it needs to get to at startup.

That's why 5W-30 or 10W-40 oils are the best. They are called "multi-weight oils," and they combine the best of both worlds. They act like a thin 5-weight oil for the cold, and like a thick 30- or 40-weight for the heat. (There are single-weight oils on the shelves, and they'll be labeled SAE 30 or SAE 40, but the multi-weights are the way to go unless your owner's manual tells you otherwise.)

One more word about oil. Your owner's manual will tell you to use an oil "rated API SJ" or above. Or SH. Or SG. The API is the American Petroleum Institute, and it sets standards for motor oils. What you'll find on store shelves is SL-rated oil. It's fine for your car. Newer protection standards—the later the letter in the alphabet—incorporate the performance properties of the earlier standards. As long as you're working up in the alphabet, you're doing right by your car.

ADDING OIL

YOU'LL NEED: OIL, PAPER TOWELS.
OPTIONAL ITEM: A FUNNEL.

1 . Adding oil is easy. While still parked somewhere flat, and with the hood open, you'll need to find the oil filler cap. It's a gas-cap-sized cap somewhere on the main central part of your engine. **(see figure B, page 13)** It should be labeled, and might even tell you what weight and grade of oil is recommended for your engine.

There are other twist-off or pop-up caps scattered around your engine compartment as well—the power steering fluid reservoir, the brake fluid reservoir, and even the windshield washer fluid reservoir—but those will all be at the edges of your engine, around the perimeter. The oil filler cap is the only one directly on the engine itself.

2 . Okay, now you've found it, open it. It'll twist loose and lift out. Set it upside down someplace flat on the engine. (You're trying to keep it clean.)

3 . Now, all you need to do is pour oil from your quart bottle into the hole where the cap was. You can do it directly out of the bottle, use a funnel, or even make a paper funnel by rolling a sheet of heavy paper into a cone—leaving the small end open for oil to flow through. Out of the bottle is easiest if you can do it without spilling. (A little spill is okay—just wipe it up with your paper towel.)

4 . Add half a quart at first, wait a moment for the oil to flow through your engine and settle at the bottom, then check the level with the dipstick again. If you're in the safe zone, great. If not, add some more. Check the dipstick again. Keep filling and checking until the oil level gets up near or at the full mark. (The reason you don't want to overfill your car with oil is that if the level gets too high it reaches up to where spinning parts are, and just like those fancy milk frothers at coffee bars, the spinning engine parts can froth your oil. Frothed oil doesn't protect your engine and tastes lousy in a latte.)

5 . Once you've got the level correct, wipe up any drips, put the cap back on tightly, close your hood, and be on your way. Save any unused oil for next time in your garage or tightly sealed in your trunk, and cap any empty containers and throw them away.

CHANGING YOUR OIL:
EVERY 5,000 MILES

This is easiest of all. Take your car to an oil changing place and pay them $20 to $40 to do it for you. You can change oil yourself, but there's no clean way to do it, and then you have to take the old oil to a recycling center. It's a pain, and you don't even really save much money. Just pay someone.

The part you need to remember is to change your oil every 5,000 miles. They used to tell you to change your oil every 3,000 miles, and not surprisingly, the oil-changing businesses still recommend having it done every 3,000 miles. Car manufacturers have raised their recommendations, some to 5,000 miles and some even up to 7,500 miles. A good compromise is every 5,000 miles, and it's also easy to remember and notice when you hit a 5 or 0 on the odometer: 30,000, 75,000, etc.

Why do you have to change your oil? Because it gets used up. Oil traps dirt and contaminants that get into your engine. If you've ever seen someone drain old oil, it's black and nasty-looking. The new oil you add is clean and light green. Oil also stops corrosive acids from building up in your engine. If you ignore oil too long, it'll no longer be able to trap and hold contaminants, and it won't stop the corrosion. Let it go too long routinely, and your engine will wear out long before it should have. Let it go indefinitely, and your engine will seize up and die. Every 5,000 miles.

TIRES

ROUND AND ROUND

If oil is the key to keeping your engine alive, tires are the key to keeping you alive. It doesn't matter how big, or fancy, or sporty, or expensive your car is, the only thing keeping it on the road is your tires. Tires today are well made, but will still lose air slowly and will eventually wear out. And if something is wrong with your car's suspension, the tires will show it. So you need to do three things with your tires: keep them inflated, look at them periodically, and replace them when they need it.

Unfortunately, you might also need to have the occasional tire repaired or flat changed. You can do it.

CHECKING AND
INFLATING YOUR TIRES

If you want to know how important it is to properly inflate your tires—which means having the right air pressure in them—flip from Emeril or MTV some Sunday and watch a NASCAR race. After a pit stop, you'll hear some crew chief with a North Carolina drawl say that they made an air pressure adjustment to improve the car's handling. These are cars flying around a track at 180 miles an hour, and to get them to steer better, they add or subtract a quarter- or half-pound of air pressure from the tires.

It's that important.

Proper inflation will have two economic benefits for you, too. It'll improve your gas mileage, and it'll make your tires last longer. (And aren't there things you'd rather spend your money on than gas and tires?)

We'll start with how much air pressure you want in your tires. Air pressure is measured in pounds per square inch, or psi, and your owner's manual will tell you the recommended inflation pressure for your tires. You will also find it on a sticker if you open the driver's door and look at the door frame. That sticker (and the manual) will tell you the right size tire to use and the right psi. Our daughter's 1995 Honda, for instance, calls for 32 psi. My wife's Hyundai

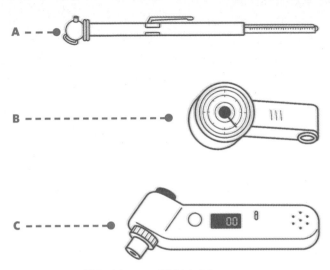

A --- Pencil Gauge (B) Dial Gauge (C) Digital Gauge

SUV recommends 30 psi for normal driving, but 32 psi if it's fully loaded with cargo and passengers. My truck is even odder: it calls for 29 psi in the front tires and 35 in the rear.

If the spare tire needs a different pressure—and many do—the sticker will also tell you that.

Just to be confusing, stamped on the tire itself will be a different number, the maximum pressure the tire can hold. That max pressure is not what you're after. You want the pressure recommended by the carmaker, so find that first.

Check your tires' air pressure before driving your car, when the tires are cold. ("Cold" just means you haven't driven on them recently, or at least haven't driven far.) As you drive, the friction between the rubber and the road heats your tires, and that heats the air inside them. As the air heats up, it expands, so you'll get a higher tire pressure reading when the tires are warm than when they're cold. (Tire manufacturers and carmakers know this, and account for it in their pressure recommendations.) So take your readings on cold tires.

You'll need a tire pressure gauge to check each tire, and you have a few choices there. First, there are usually gauges on the air hoses at gas stations (if you can still find a station with air hoses). The problem with these is that they are notoriously inaccurate, which kind of defeats the purpose.

A much better choice is buying your own gauge (or getting your parents to buy one for you—it is a safety issue after all). There are a couple of types, and you can find them at any auto parts store or supercenter. The most common are pencil-type gauges **(figure A)**. They are skinny tubes about the size, oddly enough, of a pencil. When you use them, a stick with pressure markings on it will pop out of the back end.

The second type is a dial gauge **(figure B)**. It looks like a small speedometer that plugs into your tires. When you use it, a needle will rotate around the dial and show you how much air pressure is in the tire. Both pencil and dial type gauges are pretty inexpensive—$2 to $10. Top-of-the-line brands and models are available and cost a little more.

The most accurate gauges are digital **(see figure C, page 22)**. They are powered by small batteries, and when you attach them to your tires a number will pop up on the screen telling you the air pressure. These are a little more expensive—usually in the $20 to $30 range—although you can get them on sale for about $10. What's good about digital gauges is they measure pressure down to half-pound increments, a level of accuracy you just can't get with the others. What's bad is if they break—and I've had one break—you're out $20 instead of $2.

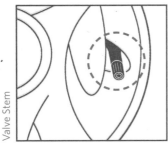

Valve Stem

1 . Whatever type you get, we'll assume you have it and your tires are cold. Go to a tire and find the valve stem. It's a little rubber tube right at the edge where the tire meets the wheel. (*Wheel* or *rim*—the terms are interchangeable.) It'll usually have a cap on it to protect the tip. Twist off the cap.

2 . Now look at your gauge. It'll have a recessed piece called a *chuck* that fits snugly over the valve stem. It'll also have a button to reset the dial or digital display. (With pencil-type gauges, you just push the stick all the way back in to reset it.) Find the reset and use it to reset the gauge to zero.

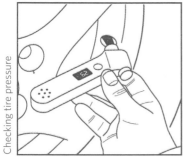

Checking tire pressure

3 . Now press the chuck firmly against the stem **(see illustration)**. If you hear the hissing sound of air escaping, you don't have a good seal, so pull the gauge off, reset it again, line up the recessed chuck straight with the stem, and try again. When you have a good seal, you'll hear an initial "wsshht" as the air pressure moves the needle or stick on your gauge, then you won't hear anything. That's what you want.

4 . Pull the gauge off the valve stem and read it. Digital and dial gauges are easy. For pencil gauges, just find the last number you can read on the stick. Be sure you're reading psi—some pencil gauges are also marked in millimeters of mercury, abbreviated Hg, and those readings will be drastically different than good old psi.

5 . If the air pressure is right, put the valve stem cap back on and move to the next tire. If it's low, check it again. (It's always a good idea to take every reading twice, just in case.) If it's still low, you'll have to use an air hose at a gas station to add air a bit at a time until it's right. If your tires are over-inflated—the pressure is higher than what's recommended—you'll have to let air out. Your tire pressure gauge will likely have a little pokey nub sticking out (a key works, too). Press that into the center of the valve stem, and you'll hear the air escaping. Let out a little at a time, and keep checking the pressure until it's right.

How close does it have to be? As close as you can get it. Being low by just one or two pounds will cost you gas mileage and tire life. Some people try to boost their gas mileage by overinflating their tires, on the assumption that if under-inflated is bad for mileage, overinflated is good. It's really not. Overinflated tires wear out faster, make your car ride stiff, and can affect your suspension. Stick with the number the carmaker put on the sticker. (Wind resistance is by far the biggest factor affecting your mileage. If you really want to improve your mileage and fuel economy, drive 55 mph.)

When you're checking your tires, check all four tires and the spare. (Trust me, you'll never feel quite as dumb as when you get a flat, get ready to change it, and then discover that your spare is flat, too.) If you have a compact spare, and most new cars do, don't freak out if the tire pressure is something like double the pressure of your regular tires. Check the door-frame sticker—you'll probably find that double is about right.

Now for the part you're not gonna like: You can't just do this once. You need to check your tires *monthly*. Pick a day that comes around every month—the first of the month, the day you pay your Visa bill, payday, whatever—and check your tires on that day. It'll take five minutes and save you hundreds of dollars over the life of your tires.

While we're on the subject, here's another reason not to listen to old-timers: Old-timers will tell you they can tell by looking at a tire whether it needs air. They can't. It used to be true, and it wasn't because old-timers were brighter back then than the rest of us are now. It was the tires. Tires back in the day were made differently and looked low when they were low. Modern radials don't. You can be significantly under-inflated and it won't show. You have to check.

TREAD WEAR
Since you're down there checking the air pressure in your tires, you might as well take a look at them, too. You can tell a lot by looking at your tires, including spotting problems that could cause a blowout, accident, or other sorts of unpleasantness.

What you want to see are tires that look like, well, tires. If everything is okay with them, you aren't going to notice anything. It's when one of the tires looks different than the others that you have problems.

SIDES

Start by looking at the side of the tire. If it's flat and black and smooth (except for the writing and numbers stamped in it), great. If you notice cracks or cuts or bubbles in the side of any of your tires, you have a big problem. Tires have belts and many layers of rubber to protect the tread area from punctures and wear. The sides of the tire don't. If you have damage to the side of any of your tires, drive slowly and carefully to a nearby tire store or garage and have somebody look at it. And be prepared to replace that tire immediately. (Don't take the car on a freeway or at freeway speeds. If there's not a tire shop within a very short distance, have the spare put on and take the damaged tire to a shop in the trunk.)

TREADS

If the sides are fine, look next at the tread. (I suppose you could call this the bottom of the tire, but does something round really have a bottom?) Just about every tire out there has a different tread pattern, but they're all designed to do pretty much the same thing—keep your tire connected to the road in a variety of road and weather conditions. The grooves force rain out of the way so the flat part of the tire can grip the road.

What you want to see when you look at the tread is uniform wear—the tire looks the same all the way across, and it looks the same as the other tires on your car. If the wear pattern is uniform—all the grooves are the same depth, all the tires look the same, and there is still some depth to the grooves, you're good to go. If the tread is worn down so your grooves are more rumors than reality, it's time for new tires. I know you don't want to spend the $200 to $600 on new tires, but you have to. Tires wear out even under perfect conditions, and replacing tires every 40,000 to 80,000 miles or so is just part of the cost of owning a car.

One way to get the most life out of your tires is to have them rotated every 10,000 miles. I know your tires are rotating all the time, but that's not what we're talking about. Rotating tires means putting the front tires on the rear and the rear ones on the front. It keeps the wear even and helps your tires last longer. It's a 20-minute, $20 job, and many tire shops do it for free if you bought your tires there. Dealers also do it as part of your regular 30,000- and 60,000-mile service.

If the wear pattern on your tires is uneven, here are some of the possible ways it might be weird and some of the reasons why. If you are checking your tires regularly, you'll be able to spot these problems early and fix them before it's so bad you have to replace individual tires. That saves you a bunch of money.

WEAR AT THE EDGES:

The center part of the tread is okay, but the edges of the tires are worn down completely—maybe even to the steel belts.

Cause:	Under inflation.	This is the classic wear pattern when you don't properly inflate your tire.

Solution: Add air to your tire.   If the wear is serious, replace the tire.

WEAR ALONG ONE EDGE OR SIDE OF THE TIRE:

Half the tire looks good, but the other half is really worn out.

Cause:	This is typically bad wheel alignment.

Your wheels are designed to face straight forward and sit straight up and down, and when you get your wheels aligned, that's exactly what the mechanics are doing. But wear or killer potholes or accident damage can knock your wheel out of alignment. It'll be slightly tipped sideways, or slightly toed in or out. So when your car is rolling, that tire isn't sitting flat and straight on the road, it's getting pushed and rubbed against the road. The road wins that battle every time, and bad alignment will chew through tires quickly.

Solution: Have your car aligned.

An alignment is typically going to cost you about as much as one tire, say $75 to $125, but it saves money in the long run. Regular tire rotations help as well.

WEAR IN THE CENTER:

The edges of the tires are okay, but the center is worn.

Cause: Over inflation.

Too much air makes your tires balloon out so only the center part touches the road.

Solution: Let air out of your tire. If the wear is bad, replace the tire.

WEAR IN CERTAIN SPOTS ON THE TIRE:

There isn't a uniform wear pattern at all. Some parts of the tire are perfect all the way across. But other spots are wearing or already worn badly.

Cause: This is likely the result of your wheels being out of balance.

No, they're not studying too much at the expense of a social life. Out of balance means there are heavy spots pulling the wheel as it spins. It's like your washing machine—put too many jeans on one side and instead of spinning smoothly, the tub is going to smack and smash against the sides. Same thing with your car. If a wheel is out of balance, the heavy part smacks the ground harder as it goes around, and the tire pays.

Solution: Have the wheel balanced at a garage or tire shop.

They do that by spinning the wheel on a special machine and attaching small lead weights to your rim opposite any heavy spots. Balancing is standard with the installation of new tires—although they do charge.

FLAT TIRES

Nobody likes flat tires, but sooner or later pretty much everybody is going to get one. Here's how to deal with it if it happens to you.

If your tire goes flat while you're driving, *do not panic*. (Unless you're going 90 mph through a mountain hairpin overlooking a 7,000-foot drop. Then panic all you want.) It may blow out with a scary bang, or it may just start to feel weird then start making a "*whup-whup-whup*" sound. Don't brake suddenly. Ease off the gas, and get off the road as soon as you safely can. If you're on a multi-lane freeway, work your way over to the right safely and steadily and then pull off the road as soon as possible. (Try to stay out of the median in the middle of the highway. It's far more dangerous in there than off to the right.)

Get as far off the roadway as you can, and try to stop someplace flat and smooth. (It makes it easier and safer when you jack the car up to change the tire.)

Now get out your cell phone and call your auto club.

They'll send help, and the driver will take off the blown tire, put on your spare, and get you on your way. New cars come with 24-hour roadside assistance. Some credit unions offer it to their members. The most well-known auto club, AAA, charges less than $50 a year for membership. It's less than the price of the Gap jeans you'll ruin changing the tire, so there's really no excuse. (Again, this is a safety issue, and I'm sure your parents love you and want you to be safe and would be happy to pay for your membership. The trick is convincing them that your cell phone is also essential safety equipment and they should pay for that, too.)

WORST-CASE SCENARIO
Your cell phone is dead, there's nobody around, and you have to deal with the flat yourself.

One way is Fix-a-Flat or some other flat-tire sealant. This is goopy stuff in a pressurized can. You screw the nozzle of the can onto your valve stem, just like if you were adding air to your tires. Press the button to dispense all the goop. If it's a small puncture, it should seal quickly and your tire will inflate. Keep that button down until the can is empty. If it works, your tire will be sealed and inflated enough to drive on slowly until you get to town. The pressure is probably way low, and you should check it and inflate it properly as soon as possible. Also, have the tire inspected and repaired at a shop. Tire sealants are emergency stopgap measures, not permanent repairs.

If the tire is too badly damaged or you don't have sealant, you'll have to change the flat yourself. You can. My sister did. (And if it's raining and the middle of the night, it'll make an even better story to tell later.)

1 . Make sure the car is in park (or in gear if it's a stick-shift). Put on your parking brake, and if there's a large rock or something lying around, put that against one of your good tires to help hold the car in place.

2 . Get the stuff you need from the trunk. You'll need your spare tire, jack, and lug wrench from the trunk. Look under the carpeting. If it's not there, look under the car. Most trucks and some cars keep their spares underneath. Find the lug wrench—it could be an X-shaped thing, or a curved metal bar with a socket head at one end that fits over your lug nuts. (Lug nuts are the things that hold your wheel on. How that also came to be a disparaging description is another Mystery.) Go to the flat tire and fit the lug wrench over the first lug nut. (Typically there are four or five.)

If you don't see any lug nuts when you look at your wheel, they're probably hidden behind a hubcap or wheel cover. Pry that off, and you should find them.

Removing lug nuts

3. Now, put the wrench over one lug nut and push like a monkey until it breaks loose. Counterclockwise is loose. (Lefty-loosy, righty-tighty.) You may have to really lean on the wrench to break the nuts loose, so be careful that your head won't smack into the fender if it happens suddenly. If it's stubborn, make sure you're pushing on the very end of the wrench to get as much leverage as you can. And be stubborn; heck, stand on the wrench if you have to. Get them all broken free and loose, but don't take them all the way off yet.

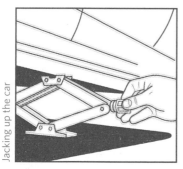

Jacking up the car

4. Now you have to jack up your car. The manual will show you the best way for your car and the jack that came with it. Most cars these days come with "scissor" jacks that raise and lower when you twist a handle rather than pump it up and down. Place the jack under the car's jacking point, a place just behind the front wheel or just in front of the back wheel.

It'll be shown in the manual. Make sure the top of the jack is directly beneath the solid frame of the car, which is usually a few inches in from the edge.

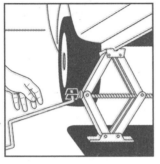

Scissor jack

If it's a scissor jack, place the bar that cranks it into the hole at the end of the threaded rod in the jack. As you turn the crank, the threaded rod brings the sides of the jack closer together, and that raises the top. Twist until the jack just touches the frame, then check to see it's centered beneath the frame and solidly set on the ground, not tippy at all. If it's all straight and solid, twist some more and raise the flat tire off the ground.

Finish twisting off the lug nuts, pull the tire straight off the wheel studs, and put it behind your car (safely out of traffic!)

5 . Now, slip the spare on, right where the regular tire was.

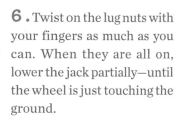

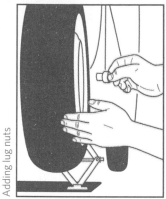

Adding lug nuts

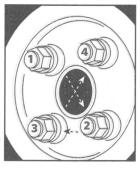

Star pattern

6. Twist on the lug nuts with your fingers as much as you can. When they are all on, lower the jack partially—until the wheel is just touching the ground.

Now twist the lug nuts down tight with the wrench. Do it in a star pattern—tighten one, then go to the loose lug nut closest to opposite it that you can. If the wheel turns, lower the jack a little more so the pressure of the ground holds the wheel still. Make sure all the lug nuts are tight. After you've cinched them down in the star pattern, do it again to be sure.

7. Now, lower the jack all the way down, tighten each nut one last time, and put all the tools and the flat tire in the trunk. If you have a mini spare—it'll look decidedly different than the tire it replaced and be labeled—you must stay below 50 mph. Mini spares aren't designed to be regular tires, and you shouldn't drive on them any more than

Tighting lug nuts

necessary. They'll get you off the highway, into town, and straight to the tire shop.

If you put rocks against your wheels to hold the car in place while you jacked it up, make sure to move them before trying to drive off, because you just used your only spare and would feel really stupid giving yourself a second flat. Drive away carefully, and get that tire taken care of that day.

TIRE REPAIRS

If you get a nail or screw in your tire, you can often have it repaired rather than having to buy a new tire. (If the sidewall is damaged, replacement is your only choice.)

If the shop says they can repair it, ask them how they do it. You want a shop that is going to take the tire off the wheel and patch it from the inside. Some shops use repair needles they insert through the puncture and go at it that way. It's cheaper and faster, but it's a lousy repair and likely to fail and leave you with another flat sometime soon. And who wants that? Spend the extra $10 to have the repair done from the inside. It should only cost you $20 or so.

NEW TIRES

Eventually you'll have to get new tires. Fortunately, there are plenty of places to buy them, from big box stores like Wal Mart and Costco to dedicated tire shops that only sell tires and wheels. If you drive a small car with small tires, yours are going to be cheaper than huge tires for a mammoth SUV or truck.

Pretty much, you'll want to replace your tires with new ones the same size. The door-frame sticker will tell you the size to put on (it's a weird sequence of numbers, like 195/60R15). Sometimes your owner's manual will list a couple of acceptable tire sizes you can use. It's important that you stick with what the manual recommends. A tire that's the wrong size can rub against your fender and wear out, throw off your speedometer readings, and even screw up your anti-lock brakes.

If you don't have or can't find your owner's manual, call a dealership and ask the service department. They'll know the right tires to buy, the right weight oil to use, and all of that stuff. They can also order a replacement manual for you.

BRAKES

STOP!

In addition to your tires, your brakes are the other critical safety component of your car. They *have* to work. If they don't feel right or are making noise, you've got to get them taken care of. Now. It won't be any cheaper to do it next week, and you could get yourself—or somebody else—big—time hurt between now and then.

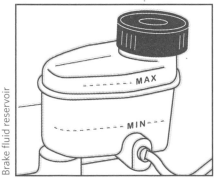

Brake fluid reservoir

We'll start with the one brake maintenance task you can do yourself—keeping an eye on the brake fluid level. (The very briefest of explanations of how brakes work: When you step on the pedal, your foot and a power booster push brake fluid through narrow hoses. At the far end of those hoses, that fluid pushes special pads against metal drums or disks attached to your wheels. The friction of those pads against the spinning drums or disks slows and stops the car. So the system needs brake fluid to work.) You'll find the brake fluid reservoir under the hood **(see figure C, page 13)**, on the driver's side at the back of the engine compartment. If you car is even remotely recent, it'll be see-through and you can tell the fluid level just by looking. If it's in the marked safe zone, you've done all the brake maintenance you need to. Close the hood and be on your way.

If the level is low (and your brakes are still working correctly), you'll need to add fluid. The cap of the reservoir will tell you what kind of fluid to add. It'll say "Use DOT 3 only" or "Use DOT 3 or 4 fluid only." It may call for DOT 5 fluid. Use what it calls for. DOT 3 and 4 fluids can be interchanged, but DOT 5 brake fluid is silicon-based and does not work in regular brake systems.

Buy a small container. Brake fluid adsorbs water vapor out of the air and goes bad when you store it even if you keep it capped. (For the same reason, don't use old brake fluid your roommate had sitting around.) Open the cap of the brake fluid reservoir and carefully pour in fresh brake fluid until the level is right. Reattach the reservoir cap, and you're done.

But be careful with brake fluid. The stuff will ruin your paint. Bad people have been known to write nasty things in brake fluid on ex-lovers' cars, permanently defacing them. (It's felony vandalism, so don't get any ideas.) Keep it away from your paint, and if you do drip any, wash it up immediately with soapy water.

If your brake fluid is low and your brakes feel spongy or you have to pump them to make the car stop, adding fluid won't be enough. (But do add the fluid.) The problem here is you have air in your brake system, and you'll have to take the car in and have a mechanic bleed the brakes. Bleeding the brakes forces out the old fluid—and any trapped air—and replaces it with new fluid. The reason you have to get the air out of your brake lines is that air compresses. If you have air in your brake system, stepping on the brake pedal doesn't force the fluid to squeeze the brake pads, it just squishes the air bubbles in the fluid. Bleeding that air out is the only way to fix it.

The other time you need to take your car into a shop is if you hear anything odd when you apply the brakes. Squealing, metallic rubbing, or maybe a rhythmic "*shhht-shhht-shhht*" that slows down as the car slows down. Those are all indications that your pads are worn, and maybe your brake disks are warped. Brakes do wear out. How fast depends a lot on where you live and how you drive, but somewhere between 60,000 and 100,000 miles, you're gonna need new brake pads. (Hopefully that's all, but rotors do wear out eventually and can get warped if they get too hot.) When your brake pads wear completely out, all you may have to stop your car is metal rubbing against metal. It's not great for stopping, and it's guaranteed to do lots and lots of expensive and unnecessary damage.

WIPER
BLADES

WHEN GOOD WIPERS
GO BAD; FILM AT 11

Here's another safety item and simple repair you can do yourself: Changing your wiper blades. They are flimsy strips of rubber and will last a year or two at the most. Fortunately, they're also cheap and easy to replace.

Buy new blades before the first rain of the year. If you wait until it is raining, like everybody else, they may not have the size you need by the time you get to the parts store. (At least it's better than the old Soviet Union. Factories there all had quotas of parts to turn out, but the quotas were based on weight, not the number of items made. So the factories made a lot of heavy items like engine cases, but light wiper blades were so scarce—and so often stolen—that nobody left them on their cars. They'd lock their wiper blades in the car until it actually started raining, then pull over and put them on.) When you go to the store and find the wiper display, it'll have a book or computer screen where you look up or enter the year and model of your car, and it tells you which wiper blades to buy. (Blades come in different lengths.)

The book may tell you that you need two different-sized wiper blades, one for the driver's side and one for the passenger's side. (And a third for the rear windshield wiper, if your car has one.) That's pretty common these days, and the driver's wiper tends to be the bigger one. If your front wipers are the same size, you can save a few bucks if you really need to. Take the passenger's side blade off and throw it away. Take the driver's side blade off and put it on the passenger's side. Then replace the driver's side blade with a new one. Since you look out of the driver's side of the windshield almost exclusively, you can get away with just changing that blade most of the time. (If your blades are different sizes, this doesn't work, of course.)

When you buy blades, you'll have another option besides length. You'll be able to choose whether you just replace the rubber strip itself—which is cheaper—or the whole wiper arm assembly, strip and all. If your wiper arms aren't damaged and there aren't big gaps under the wipers that aren't getting clean, replacing just the rubber strip is usually all you need.

YOU'LL NEED: NEW WIPER BLADES THAT FIT YOUR CAR.
To replace the strips, lift up your wiper blade arm until it stays up by itself, then take a look at it. The rubber wiper is set in a strip of plastic that has grooves in the sides. Those grooves slide onto the arm. At the end, there will be two springy tabs shaped like arrowheads. Those slip past a tab on the wiper arm and lock the blade into place. To remove it, simply squeeze those arrowheads together with your fingers and push the blade off the arm. Once you get the arrows past the tab, it'll just slide out.

To install the new blade, just line up the tabs on the arm with the grooves on the blade and slide the blade into place. Make sure the arrows go past the last tab to lock the blade into place. (If it's not locked in place, it'll work itself off the wiper arm as you use it.)

If you're replacing the whole wiper arm, the packaging will include a clasp and instructions on how to detach the old wiper arm and lock the new one in place. (Different brands clasp in different ways.) It's easy and doesn't require any tools.

You can also buy and have wipers installed at any garage, and many full-service gas stations. It'll typically cost you double the price of doing it yourself.

ADDING WASHER FLUID

While we're on the subject, there's one more windshield-related maintenance task you ought to take care of: adding washer fluid. This is the easiest car-maintenance task there is. The fluid itself is cheap—$1 or $2 for a gallon bottle at any gas station, discount store, or auto parts store. (The only decision you may have to make depends on whether you live someplace really dang cold. If so, look for washer fluid that says it doesn't freeze. Otherwise, just grab whatever they have.)

Open your hood (see illustration, page 12) and find the windshield washer fluid filler cap. It's often in the front left and usually labeled. Pop open the cap, pour in fluid until it reaches the full mark, and close the cap. Save the rest of the fluid for the next time you need it, and try not to let the washer fluid run completely out in your car.

WASHING AND WAXING

SPA TREATMENTS

Keeping your car clean and shiny not only makes it (and you) look good, it helps protect your car and may help you get a better price for it when you eventually sell it. So here's the quick and dirty guide to washing your car.

WASHING
YOU'LL NEED: CAR WASH SOAP, WATER, A SOFT SPONGE, AND COTTON TOWELS.
Yes, you can go to a drive-through wash, or pay a few bucks extra for an all-hand wash. The do-it-yourself places with their high-pressure hoses aren't the best thing for your paint, but they are cheap and quick.

If you want to wash your car yourself, buy some car wash soap. Dish soap is too harsh for auto paint, believe it or not.

(Which makes sense when you think about it. Dishes aren't painted: they're glazed. Dish soap makers don't have to worry about damaging paint. Car soap makers do.) Add the recommended amount of soap to cool water, hose off your car with a gentle spray, and wash it down with your sponge. (I like to have one sponge that's just for washing cars, and it stays in my car-washing bucket. If you use it for general cleaning, you can embed dirt in it and scratch your paint.) Try not to do it in direct sun in 105-degree heat. Rinse as you go so the soap doesn't dry on your paint, and when you're finished, lightly dry the car with soft towels so you don't get water spots. It's about a 20-minute job for a quick wash, longer if you're really gonna go after it and do the interior, tires, etc.

WAXING
YOU'LL NEED: WAX, AN APPLICATOR,
AND A SOFT, DRY TOWEL.
Car wax is like SPF 30 sunscreen. You can go without it, but you'll pay for it down the road. Keeping your car waxed will do more to preserve its finish than anything else.

Waxing isn't fun, but it's not sans-anesthesia dental work either. It'll take about an hour, and doing it once every two to three months will really keep your car's finish protected. You don't go out without skin protection, do you?

1 . There are different types of waxes, but most go on the same way. You rub a small amount of wax—about a dime-sized blob—onto the painted parts of your car with a soft applicator. It'll cover an area about two by two feet—a fender perhaps.

2 . Let the wax dry to a haze. When it's dry, rub it away with your towel. Refold the towel frequently so you're using a clean part of it. It takes some work to rub out the wax, so consider it your workout for the day. Work in small areas, try to keep the wax out of nooks and crannies where it's hard to wipe away, and never wax your car in hot direct sun. (The wax will bake on before you have a chance to wipe it off, and it can ruin the finish. My dad had a baby-blue 1964 Chevy Impala with permanent white wax swirls in it after I broke that rule when I was 11.)

That's about it. Keep your car washed, and every three or four washings give it a nice wax. Then in five or ten years, you can still sell it on looks rather than just telling people how reliable and economical it is.

There are a lot of other car-care products out there, everything from upholstery cleaners to dashboard protectors to tire shiners, and you can use as many or as few of them as you want.

REPAIRS

$@%#! HAPPENS

Things break. That's just the way it is. But there are folks out there who can fix them. When your car breaks, you want to take it to a mechanic who is honest, competent, and reliable. Many are. Unfortunately, some aren't and as a result mechanics in general have a bad reputation and make people nervous. So how do you find a good mechanic or recognize a good mechanic when you do find one? Good question.

THE DEALERSHIP VS. INDEPENDENT MECHANICS

When your car needs repair or service, you have two basic options: take it to a dealer or to an independent garage. There are pros and cons to both.

DEALERSHIPS

We'll start with dealerships. Your dealer's service department has more expertise fixing your brand of car than anybody since it's pretty much all they see. If there's a short-cut—a removing-this-bracket-gives-better-access-to-that-bolt kind of thing—they'll know it. They'll recognize the warning signs of common problems. They get the latest information—repair updates and service bulletins—and have all the specialty tools needed to fix your car. If the repair is under warranty, they're the only ones who can fix it.

So what's the downside? Price can be one. Dealership work is expensive. If the repair is major or your car is older, it may simply be too costly to have it done there.

Availability is another issue. If the nearest dealership is 60 miles away, having your car fixed there may not be your best bet.

There is also work dealership shops will do and work they won't do. Let's say you've worn out your 1989 Acura Integra's engine after 220,000 miles. But your uncle's neighbor has one that was rear-ended and wrecked with only 89,000 miles on the engine. You'll be able to find an independent mechanic who will swap those engines. Don't count on a dealership doing that work.

One final word about dealerships. They are no more or less honest than anyone else. Some are great. They'll only do the work you need and treat you fairly and well. Others aren't such straight shooters. If you run across a bad dealership, complain to the carmaker. Write to their customer service department. Carmakers want the people who buy and drive their cars to like their cars and recommend them to all their friends, and a bad dealership hurts the brand.

INDEPENDENT MECHANICS

Okay, now let's talk about independent mechanics. Independent mechanics are guys like Al down at Al's Garage. They'll fix anything you bring in and will usually tackle any repair, large or small.

We'll start with the advantages. Independent mechanics are everywhere. There may not be a dealership for 100 miles, but there will be a garage. Price is another factor. Since most garages have lower overhead than a dealership, they also have lower labor rates. (And it's typically the labor that really gets you in any major repair.) Most mechanics are certified, and all of them like buying tools, so chances are they'll have the skill and equipment to handle your repair. And many of them are genuinely nice guys who will take good care of you.

The downsides of independent garages is that they may not have the latest service and repair bulletins from your car maker, and they won't be able to do warranty work. (At least not for free.)

And then there are the bad apples. They'll tell you things are broken when they're not and sell you a whole radiator when all you need is a thermostat. And while you can (and should) complain to your state's licensing bureau, Better Business Bureau, and even the local District Attorney's office if you get clipped by a shady mechanic, there isn't a major car manufacturer he's relying on for inventory who will twist his arm and get him to clean up his act.

SPECIALTY REPAIR

There is one more repair option worth mentioning—the specialty repair shops, which include national chains. These are muffler shops, transmission shops, brake shops, radiator shops, and body shops. If what you need is what they do, specialty shops can be a good way to go.

FINDING A GOOD MECHANIC

So how do you find a good mechanic when you need one?

Ask.

Ask the car nuts you know—guys or gals who spend too much time and money on their rides. Ask folks who drive the same make car as you do. (Even if they're people you just saw in a parking lot for the first time.) Call and ask your good mechanic back in your hometown if he or she knows and can recommend anyone out where you are now.

There's a good website to check, too. It's www.cartalk.com, the website of the guys who do the *Car Talk* radio show on

NPR. One of the links on their site is labeled Mechan–X Files, and Car Talk listeners across the country recommend good mechanics and good shops. Put in your zip code and see who's recommended in your area. (And if you have a good mechanic, go onto the site and recommend him or her.)

HERE'S WHAT TO LOOK FOR:
What if your taking a shot in the dark? A good mechanic will explain what's wrong and tell you why it went wrong. He or she will tell you what you absolutely have to do, and what you can afford to wait to do. He or she will know you're not an expert in auto repair and won't make you feel stupid. A good mechanic won't pressure you and won't mind if you take your car somewhere else for a second opinion. (If you do, and the second shop tells you the same thing, it's good karma to go back to the shop where you started unless you felt there was something wrong with that shop.)

Every mechanic should give you a written estimate of the work and the price before beginning repairs and call you for authorization if he or she finds something else wrong during the repair. State laws vary, but in some states you have a right to ask for and be given the bad parts that came off your car. (The idea is that if they've replaced a part that didn't need to be, you've got a way to tell.) Some people just use the parts to make interesting paperweights or mobiles. Or gifts! Wouldn't your little brother just love a used timing chain for Christmas?

Basically, finding a good mechanic is just a matter of good shopping. And while you may not know much about cars, most everybody knows how to shop.

CHAPTER 2:

COMPUTERS

Computers are among the most wonderful and frustrating inventions on the planet. They work tremendously well most of the time, but when a computer messes up, there are few things as uncooperative. This chapter will cover the basics on keeping your computer alive and well, and keeping it (and you) safe from the bad things and people skulking out there in cyberspace.

Let's start with a general principle that applies to your computer, as well as your car, bicycle, and just about any other device out there: Nothing works perfectly forever without maintenance. Just as you have to change the oil and check the tire pressure in your car, you have to perform a few chores to keep your computer in tip-top shape. The good news is, you won't get greasy doing any of them (unless you do them really, really wrong.)

Let's start with the really bad stuff.

VIRUSES

NOT YOUR AVERAGE BIRD FLU

Viruses are nasty little computer programs that are designed to sneak into your computer and then do something bad—like delete the contents of your hard drive, for instance. Like a real virus, these malicious programs need to spread to survive, so they will often also try to hijack your e-mail and send themselves to all your friends, IM buddies, and professors. (Not a happy way to get yourself recognized in class.) There are similar programs called *worms* that do the same thing and are almost as bad.

You don't want either on your computer. Trust me.

So, your first computer chore is to make sure there is a current anti-virus program installed and running on your machine. This one isn't so hard these days because as computer viruses have caused more havoc, Internet services, software companies, businesses, and colleges have all become better at trying to keep viruses off their systems.

A couple of the big anti-virus programs are Symantec's Norton Anti-Virus and McAfee's VirusScan, which you can buy at Office Depot, any office supply store, or download directly from the companies' websites. (It's not free if you download it—you still have to pay.) Some colleges have licenses for Norton or other anti-virus programs and not only provide them free to their students, they insist that you install the program before letting you onto the college computer network. Check with your college. Or check with your employer—the company you work for may have a similar deal and will protect your home computer in order to protect their office systems. Some Internet service providers also give their customers free access to these programs, so it's worth checking. (And if you're choosing between two ISPs and one provides free anti-virus software and the other doesn't, factor that in. Buying them yourself costs $50 a year or so.)

What makes anti-virus programs valuable is constant updating. Anti-virus programs work by recognizing the specific lines of computer code that make viruses and worms work. When they spot that code, the anti-virus program throws up a big shield to keep the program from infecting your computer. You need a program that updates itself automatically because pencil-neck virus writers are always trying to out-smart the anti-virus programs and come up with new infectious codes the programs don't recognize yet. The good guys stay on the lookout for these new virus codes and send out updates to all their users so their computers will recognize the new viruses.

What this means for you is that when you install your anti-virus software, you need to set it to update itself automatically. Once you've done that, you are pretty well good to go. The program itself will tell you if there is a problem, and it will remind you in a year when you have to renew your subscription to the service. Also, schedule your anti-virus software to scan your computer weekly. Pick a time when the computer is usually on and you're not there, and just let it do its thing. Hopefully, it'll never find a single virus on your system. If it does, it'll give you a choice of deleting the file outright or keeping it in quarantine. There aren't many good reasons to quarantine a virus-corrupted file. Personally, I don't want virus-infected files anywhere on my system, so I always choose to delete the files permanently.

Symantec and McAfee aren't the only companies that make good anti-virus software. A couple of companies that make commercial anti-virus products give a version away for home users, figuring they'll make their money selling to businesses. Avast is one such company, and home users can download a free version of their anti-virus software from www.avast.com. You have to register and give them an e-mail address, and they send a registration code that unlocks the program and makes it work. Avast's program updates itself and does a good job of protecting your computer.

Viruses tend to come in waves, so if your roommates or friends get a virus, be extra, extra careful, especially about opening e-mails with attachments. If you don't recognize the sender, just delete the e-mail. If it came from a friend, you can always e-mail back and ask if they sent you something before you open the suspicious e-mail. And, if you have access to a public computer at school or a library, you can always open the e-mail there through a web-mail program to see if it's really legit. If it is, you can open it safely on your home computer. If it's not, delete it through the web-mail system, and it won't have done you any harm.

Most computer viruses target computers running Microsoft software, both the Windows operating software (which makes your computer work) and Internet Explorer. The reason for this is that so many more computers work on Microsoft software than any other, so virus writers get more bang for their buck. For Macs, this is a selling point. (As if the cute commercials weren't enough.) Some folks have also begun using alternative operating systems or browsers to avoid viruses. Some folks have also begun using alternative operating systems or browsers to avoid viruses. Picking a new browser is easy–Firefox, Opera and Chrome are all popular and readily available–but running an alternative operating system can get way geeky way quick. Stick with the operating system you have and let a good anti-virus program take care of the rest.

SPYWARE AND ADWARE

SPIES

Almost as nasty as viruses, spyware and adware are two other types of malicious programs that can infect your computer. Spyware is the most sinister. It lurks in the background and can record everything you do at your keyboard—like type in passwords and account numbers—and then send that information to somebody else. Adware is less dangerous but more annoying. Adware programs make your computer work against you. They hijack Internet searches, sending you to the sites they want you to see, and they will keep those annoying pop-up ads popping up even if you have a pop-up blocker working. (In fact, getting pop-ups despite a working pop-up blocker is a good way to know your computer is infected.) A bunch of adware will also slow your computer way down.

So how does adware get onto your machine? Like a vampire, you pretty much have to invite it in. It'll come along with free downloads from the Internet tacked on to those cute fishy icons or smileys or free search toolbars. My advice? Don't download cutesy crap. Don't click on links in unsolicited e-mails or pop-up windows. (Even the buttons in pop-ups that say "close." Use the X in the top right of the window to close it.) Don't shoot the clown in banner ads. Don't think someone is gonna give you a free iPod or laptop or TV, because they're not.

Many anti-virus programs include anti-spyware protection. If yours doesn't, Yahoo makes a good program that combats spyware and adware, and it's a free download. (And it's an exception to the rule above.) From Yahoo, download the Yahoo toolbar, which includes a pop-up blocker and anti-spyware. Run the anti-spy program every few days at first—it only takes a minute or so. The first time, it'll probably find a bunch of stuff. It'll give you choices on what to do with the programs, and you should choose to remove it all. The first time, the program may not be able to remove all traces of every adware program. Restart your computer, run anti-spy again, and usually it'll get them the second time.

Sometimes you have to remove them yourself. Your system will have an "Add or remove programs" function that shows you a list of all the programs loaded on your computer. Unfortunately, the adware and spyware programs in that list aren't going to say "adware" and "spyware." They're going to have more innocent-sounding names, like Hotbar Search Assistant. Or they are going to have the same names as the programs that your anti-spy program wasn't able to remove. If you see those names, click on them then click "remove" and wait for the computer to do its thing. You may have to follow some prompts, and some programs try to convince you to leave them installed. (Adware that begs—it's so shameful.)

You should recognize most of the programs on the list as the stuff you use—Adobe Reader, your anti-virus program, Microsoft Office, etc. Try to remove all the obvious adware junk, but be careful not to remove a program you use and need. Restart your computer, run anti-spy again, and see what it finds. If you're still getting adware that the program can't remove, it's time to call your roommate's geeky kid brother (or an actual trained technician) to get rid of it.

SPAM

DELICIOUS AND NUTRITIOUS

I hate spam. I don't want online Viagra (or a big reason to buy it) or any of the other tonics, potions, schemes, or crap spammers want me to buy. If you feel the way I do, here are some ways you can reduce the clutter in your inbox.

First, never click on a link in a spam e-mail. If you do that, you tell the spammers that your address is valid and you're the kind of person who opens spam e-mail, and then look out Nellie! You'll have to change your e-mail to escape it.

Second, pick an Internet Service Provider that has a good spam filter and make sure it's set up when you open an account. If your spam filter is working, most of the junk e-mail that finds you will get weeded out and either killed outright or put into a junk mail folder. (You'll have to access your web-mail to see the junk mail folder. If you've set up an e-mail program like Outlook Express to handle your e-mail, the spam is getting cleaned off without your ever seeing it.) It's a good idea to check your junk mailbox once in a while. Occasionally an e-mail you want will get sent there (especially e-mails from companies.) The web-mail should give you a way to tell it that a certain message is not spam. Do it, then the next time you get an e-mail from that company it'll get through. (The reverse is true, too. If a spam slips through to your inbox, tell your web-mail program that it was spam so the filter will catch it the next time.)

Don't tell anyone I told you, but you can also tell your e-mail handler that those messages from your crazy Aunt Ida or whiny, high-maintenance ex are also spam, and you'll never see them again.

Another strategy for avoiding spam is creating disposable e-mail accounts. I have my main e-mail that I use with friends and folks I deal with regularly. But when I want to take an online survey, or subscribe to a site, or enter a contest, I do not use my main e-mail. (Not even when I downloaded the Avast anti-virus software.) My Internet provider lets me have up to 10 active e-mail addresses, so I created a second one, steve2nd@, that I used for stuff like that. It eventually started getting a bunch of spam, while my main e-mail stayed spam-free. When steve2nd got too buried, I deactivated it and created steve3rd. (I also do not link these accounts with my Outlook Express e-mail program. I only check them online.) It's an easy way to avoid the worst of the spam.

Also, even if you're using a throw-away e-mail, uncheck the box that says "Please send me special offers and information." The translation for that is, "Please fill my inbox with an unbelievable amount of crap I'll never need."

One more spam suggestion: Don't put your primary address on a website. Any website. There are programs out there that do nothing but scan websites looking for e-mail addresses to send spam to.

SAFE COMPUTING

DOING IT SAFELY

One time, I watched a young lady goofing around on the Internet at the end of a class. (The fact that it was my class didn't bother me—she was done with her test and killing time.) She was visiting a Rob Zombie–related website and had already entered her name and address, and when it asked her to enter her Social Security number to verify her age, she dutifully did.

This is dumb, people.

Do not give out your Social Security number willy-nilly. The only time you'll be legitimately asked for it is when you're applying for credit, opening a bank account, or doing anything tax-related. The rest of the time, if someone asks for your Social Security number, tell them to take a hike.

Why? Because it is the one thing people need to know to apply for credit. Say I'm a bad guy who would rather steal for a living than work. I could go rob banks or hold up jewelry stores, but there's that potential inconvenience of prison, getting shot, or exploding dye packs. Instead, I set up a website that attracts young and trusting visitors. With very legitimate-sounding reasons, I ask my young and trusting visitors for their names, addresses, and Social Security numbers. Being young and trusting, they give them.

I now have all I need to apply for store credit cards, bank credit cards, car loans, gas cards, bank accounts, and just about any other type of credit you can think of. Maybe I need to make a fake ID with your name on it to use them all, maybe not.

I go to Kay Jewelers and open a charge account—in your name—to buy a $1,200 diamond ring. I pawn the ring for $700 and pocket the cash, and a month later, you get the bill. You'll also be getting one from Victoria's Secret, Sears, and Texaco. By the time you've figured it out, I've stopped using your name and have moved on to someone else. Your credit is ruined, I'm afraid, and you'll have the devil's own time making it all right.

So, do not give out personal information over the Internet, not unless you're dang sure who is asking and that the request is legitimate. If you have any doubts, call the company or government agency who is asking. (People do still do business over the phone, you know.) Don't give out your Social Security number, your checking account number, or, most importantly from my point of view, your parents' checking account number.

What about shopping online? If it's a big and well-know retailer, Amazon.com for instance, yeah, it's as safe as it's going to get. If the site isn't well-known, you want to make sure it is a secure site. Three ways to tell. One, the site will (somewhere) tell you whether or not it's secure and your data will be encrypted when you send it. While there's no perfect encryption, it's a heck of a lot harder to swipe your credit card number when it's encrypted than when it's not. Also, look at the web address. A secure site will have an address that begins "https://" rather than just "http://" (That "s" is the important part.) Finally, look at the menu bar at the bottom of the page. A secure site will have a little pad-lock icon down there. An insecure site won't.

PUBLIC
COMPUTERS

DOING IT SAFELY IN PUBLIC

A quick word about public computers, the ones at school or work or in an Internet cafe. Public computers are a lot like public bathrooms—you can do your business on them, but it's good to take a few extra precautions.

Does the computer have spyware on it that will record any information you type in? Maybe. So it may be okay to check your e-mail, but not to do any online banking. (One of the places I work is rampant with viruses and spyware, so I always run an anti-spy and anti-virus scan before I start working, and I still don't access my online bank or credit card accounts from that computer.)

Some e-mail and other programs will ask if you want them to remember your passwords when you log on. Handy on your home machine, not so bright to do on a public machine.

Finally, depending on the setup, the person who uses the computer after you may be able to see and access whatever websites you just visited. To make that impossible, wipe your tracks before you leave. Before you exit the web browser, clear your browsing history. It'll wipe away your online fingerprints and the next person to use the computer won't know the websites you just visited.

SOCIAL NETWORKING SITES

MY, WHAT A PRETTY FACEBOOK YOU HAVE

Another safety issue to remember is that whatever you post online—in a blog or on your MySpace or Facebook pages—is essentially available for anyone to see at any time forever.

I know it's not supposed to be that way, but it really is. There are companies that make money linking postings and usernames to real people. The government has been inhaling all our Internet activity—including your postings and e-mails—and won't tell anybody what it's doing with them.

The good news is young folks are more tuned in to the security features of MySpace and Facebook than their parents (no surprise there . . .) and are more likely to limit their pages to friends. So just be careful. Before you post that picture—with your name attached to it—ask what you'd say about it in five years if it comes up during a job interview. If it's going to be a hard thing to explain away, rethink putting it up. (At least don't tag it with real names.) Not long ago a student-teacher got fired and kicked out of her college when a principal (or busybody parent) came across a picture she posted that had been taken at a Halloween party. In the photo, she's wearing a pirate hat and drinking from a straw. You can't see what she's drinking. You can't tell her blood alcohol level from a photo. But the caption "Drunken Pirate" was enough excuse for her school district to fire her.

Fair warning.

HARD DRIVE MAINTENANCE

CLEANING UP AFTER YOURSELF

One time when I was visiting my daughter in Santa Barbara, she asked me to take a look at her computer because it was running slowly. In addition to a ridiculous number of adware and spyware programs cluttering up her system, her 60 gigabyte hard drive was something like 97 percent full. This was on a computer just a few months old. (To put it in perspective, my 5-year-old computer at home has a 55 gigabyte hard drive that's only 20 percent full.)

When you let your hard drive get that full, the computer has a hard time finding space to save new documents or programs, which makes things slower. It also ends up splitting those documents up into little pieces—putting a bit of it here, a bit there, and the rest back here on your hard drive.

That also slows things down, because when you tell the computer to open the document, it has to find it in all those different places.

So, don't clutter up your hard drive.

On my daughter's machine, the problem was the movies and music files she'd downloaded. (I have no evidence that those downloads were illegal or violated anyone's copyright, and anyway, she's out of the country now.) Audio and especially video files are huge, and they will fill up your computer faster than a shopaholic can fill up a sale bag at an Old Navy clearance.

This is going to sound like a safe-sex lecture for a moment, so bear with me. When it comes to downloading music and movies without paying for them, the best practice really is abstinence. Make any rationalization you want, but in the end it's still stealing. You are taking something you should pay for and getting it free. It's no better than shoplifting, burglary, or grand theft auto.

If the moral argument doesn't work, consider the legal one: You may get sued, fined, or prosecuted. (The more you download, the greater the chances the recording or movie industries will come after you.) Courts have held that the software companies that create the peer-to-peer software that makes illegal downloading so easy can be held responsible for the piracy of the people who use the software, so don't be surprised if peer-to-peer file sharing networks start cracking down or shutting down.

And keep in mind that there are legal and cheap ways to download music. Getting songs for $1 each isn't unreasonable, and new subscription services are even cheaper if you need a lot of music. (Just a side note: Software companies are also cracking down on copied and "cracked" versions of their programs. Think twice about buying or borrowing software from the guy in the trench coat down the hall.)

If abstinence isn't your thing and you're too much of a tightwad to pay to download stuff legitimately, at least be smart about it. (This is the "If-you're-going-to-do-it-anyway, at-least-do-it-safely" part of the lecture....) Make sure your anti-virus program is updated. Then, after you've downloaded something, get the huge files off your hard drive. Burn movies to DVDs. Media storage is cheap and easy, and there is no reason to fill up your entire hard drive with a bunch of media files that can be better stored elsewhere.

CLEANING UP AND DEFRAGMENTING

There are two final easy maintenance tasks you need to keep up on. These are every-month-or-two tasks, and they're not too revolting to do.

CLEANING THE HARD DRIVE

The first is to clean up your hard drive. Your computer will have a utility program that scans your hard drive looking for unnecessary files to delete or compress. When you start it, it'll take a few minutes to scan your hard drive, then give you several options of things to delete or compress. (Those options will usually be in the form of a check box. Check the items you want deleted, uncheck the ones you want to keep.) I delete downloaded program files, temporary Internet files, and offline web pages. I don't delete Office setup files, because if I ever need to reload the Office software or add to it, they'll come in handy. I also tell the program to delete files in the recycle bin, temporary files, and web client/publisher temporary files. Compression is okay, but not necessary unless you really need the space.

DEFRAGMENTING

Once you've cleaned up your drive, it's time to defragment it. The reason you want to defragment your hard drive is because, as you now know, your computer doesn't necessarily keep programs and documents all together on the disk. What defragmenting does is take all those bits of saved files that were broken apart and put them together in order in one place. Then it's easier and faster for your computer to access those files.

So find or use a utility program called a disk defragmenter. It's included in Windows, not with Macs. (Do this after a disk cleanup, because the disk cleanup will free up the space for putting the files all together.) A screen will come up, giving you two choices—analyze and defragment. Analyze first. You computer will scan its hard drive and show you how much of your hard drive is used and how fragmented files are. (If you've never done this before, it can be ugly the first time.) When the analysis is done, the computer will tell you one of two things: You should defragment this volume (the hard drive), or it's not necessary to defragment at this time. Follow its recommendation (although defragmenting a drive that doesn't really need it yet doesn't hurt, it's just not necessary).

It takes a while, and if you watch the display window you'll see the computer moving the fragmented bits around until the files are whole and on one part of the hard drive. It's not quite as exciting as watching paint dry, but is better than watching grass grow. You can certainly ignore it and keep working, or use defragmenting time as a perfect excuse to catch up on some quality TV.

Unfortunately, there are still a whole bunch of things that can go wrong with your computer, but hopefully they rarely will. If something else weird does come up, call in an expert.

CHAPTER 3:

BICYCLES

As far as bikes are concerned, there are really just three things you absolutely need to know: How to set your seat, how to keep your chain lubricated, and how to fix a flat. Beyond that, if anything goes wrong with your bike, take it to a bike shop and let one of the multiply-pierced mechanics there fix it. (Why bike mechanics have so many piercings is also a Mystery, but may be somehow psychologically linked to punctured tubes back in their childhoods.)

THE SEAT

SIT ON IT!

Getting your seat set right is more than just a matter of comfort, although comfort is a very important part of the equation. It's also a safety issue.

Let's start with what the right height is. If you can sit on your bike seat and put both feet flat on the ground, your seat is too low. You don't need to put both feet flat on the ground while you ride, and having it that low is bad for your knees.

If you can't reach the ground at all, it's too high. That's an easy one.

You want your seat set where you can reach the ground with your toes when you sit on the bike. As you pedal, your leg should be bent just a little at the bottom of the pedal stroke. Road racers take this extremely seriously and set their seats to the millimeter to get the absolute most-efficient position they can on their bikes. (They also ride 140 miles a day over 9,000-foot mountains, wear brightly colored Lycra, shave their legs, and debate whether to wear their sunglasses outside their helmet straps or inside the straps, so we're pretty much gonna write them off as insane anyway.) You just want your seat height to be close and comfortable, and having it a little too low is better than a little too high.

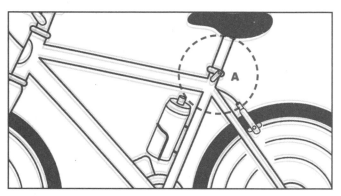

SETTING THE RIGHT HEIGHT

If your seat height is off, it's easy to adjust. Take a look below the seat. It's attached to a post, and that post sticks into your bike frame and is clamped in place. (Bike makers build them this way so seats can be adjusted.) What you're looking to find out is how the seat post is secured to the frame. The clamp will be held one of two ways: held by a quick-release, or held by a bolt. You're hoping for a quick-release **(see figure A)**.

Quick releases were invented by an Italian bike racer who couldn't get a wheel off during a freezing race over the Alps because his hands were too cold. After the race, he devised an ingenious way around the problem and went on to fame and fortune as a bicycle components builder.

You can tell if you have a quick-release if there's a lever. So, look at your frame where the seat post goes in. It'll have a clamp right at the top of the frame. If there's a lever on one side of that clamp, it's a quick-release. Pry that lever open (with your fingers, a screwdriver, or a neighbor), and the clamp will loosen. Pull or push the seat post up or down to get the seat to the right height, then push the lever back down. (Spinning it will only increase or decrease the amount of force it takes to open and close the lever. It will not tighten the clamp.) When it's locked into place, take a ride and test it out. If you're happy, cool. If not, open the quick-release and adjust it again.

What if there's no lever? If that's the case, there will be a bolt. Some will just have a bolt, some will have a nut and a bolt. Take a look at yours. If there's just a bolt, chances are it's an Allen-head bolt—it's round and has a hexagon-shaped hole in the top of it. (These are also called hex bolts.) To loosen it you'll need a hex wrench that fits into that hole. It'll probably be a 5mm or 6mm hex wrench, and they are sold at supercenters, hardware stores, and bike shops for next to nothing. (Also, if there's a hex bolt on the seat clamp of your bike, there will a dozen more in various other places, so it's worth having the one tool that will tighten them.)

Some older and cheaper bikes have a standard nut-and-bolt arrangement. The outside of both are hexagonal, and you'll need a tool that fits around them to loosen and tighten them. The best tools for the job would be a box-end wrench on the bolt and a socket on the nut. (See the Tools chapter, page 228.) However, you can get the job done with a couple of open-end adjustable wrenches. (These are commonly called crescent wrenches, for reasons that will be explained later.)

To adjust your seat, fit one crescent wrench around the nut (the small piece that threads onto the long bolt) and the other onto the head of the bolt. Twist the nut counterclockwise to loosen it. You don't need to take it all the way off. Just loosen it enough to be able to slide the seat post up and down. Set it where you want it, then tighten the nut down. (You want it tight enough so the seat post can't slip, but don't go crazy. Over-tightened nuts cause really ugly problems.)

Test it out, and if you're happy, you're done. If not, try again. The good thing about setting the seat height is that it really is a one-time deal. Once you get it dialed in, you'll never have to do it again.

SETTING THE SEAT ANGLE: AHHHH OR AGONY

Seats can also be adjusted to tip up or down. This isn't a safety issue, but if you've ever ridden on a seat set at the wrong angle, you know it can be an agony issue. There are few common household items more uncomfortable than a poorly adjusted bicycle seat.

How do you know whether your seat is set at the right angle? Ride your bike for 15 minutes. If your seat-sitting parts are in serious pain or numb, the angle may be wrong *for you*. (The seat may be wrong as well, but we'll start with the angle.) Notice that I said the angle may be wrong for you. There is no right or proper seat angle. Bodies differ, and what works for one person can be torture for another.

Look under your seat, and you'll see how the angle adjustment works. The post that connects your seat to the bike bolts to a couple of rails on the seat itself. That connection is adjustable, so you can loosen it, tip the seat up or down slightly, then retighten it.

This will take a wrench to loosen the adjusting nut under the seat, and possibly a second wrench to hold the bolt still while you loosen and tighten the nut. (If the seat tips at all when you sit on it, the nut isn't tight enough.)

If your seat wasn't level, start by setting it level and try that. Some people like a seat tipped slightly up. For others, this is a position only slightly less excruciating than sitting naked on broken glass. Some people prefer the front of the seat slightly tipped down. Most are okay with flat, or close to flat.

If you've tried several variations and there is no comfortable way to set your seat, try a different seat. There are hundreds of different seats out there, just like there are hundreds of different butts, and some seats fit some butts better than others. Just remember that the first few times riding a bike are going to include a little discomfort no matter how perfect everything is, so don't rush into any major purchases or changes. Let your body get used to it a few days, then make whatever changes you need to.

BUYING A SEAT

The best way to buy a new seat is to ride your bike to the local bike shop and let the folks there help you. You can buy a seat at Target or any supercenter and hope it fits better than the one you have (and it may), but at a bike shop the folks will usually take a little time and put in a little effort to get you a seat that will work for you.

If it's not comfortable, they can switch it out right there. Be prepared to pay a few extra bucks for the time and effort, but it's worth it to ride in comfort.

BIKE CHAINS

JUST CHAINS, NO WHIPS

If the only upkeep you ever perform on your bicycle is lubing your chain, you're doing okay. It's the one chore you absolutely have to do. (Unless you like riding around squeaking like a big rusty hinge everywhere you go until it eventually breaks when you're four miles from home on the hottest day of the year.)

Lubing your chain is also simple. First, you'll need some chain lube. They sell it at any bike shop and any sporting goods store with a bike section. Wal Mart, K-mart, and Target all have bike lube, and if you don't have any of those around, you can get stuff that'll work—WD-40—at a hardware store. (If this book teaches you nothing else, hopefully it'll convince you to buy WD-40. WD-40 isn't the world's best chain lube—it's too thin for that—but it will at least keep your chain from rusting until you go out and buy real chain lube.)

The lube you get will either be a liquid that you drip onto the chain or an aerosol spray you squirt onto the chain. Either is fine, but you tend to get more for your money with the drip-on liquids. Bike shops sell different kinds of lubes, some oil-based, some waxed-based. For most purposes, oil-based are best and usually cheaper. (Wax lubes are only better if you ride in really dusty conditions—like dry forest roads in the summer.)

Here's what you do. If you can spin your pedals backward, you can do it all yourself. If your bike has coaster brakes—the kind where you push the pedals backward to brake—it's easier with a friend. For the moment, we'll assume you can spin the pedals backward. Lean your bike against a wall or a tree and put your kickstand up. Spin your pedals backward to make sure you can go all the way around without hitting the wall or the tree.

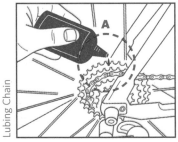

Lubing Chain

Now put the tip of the lube bottle over the chain (see figure A). Make sure it's right over the top of the chain, not off to the side. Spin the pedals backward slowly and drip lube out in a slow stream so it gets onto each and every link in the chain. You are trying to get the lube on all the pins, the small bars that connect the sides of the chain. Spin the chain around so it goes through the lube twice. (Make sure to get the whole chain. It will take several revolutions of the pedals.)

Once it's all lubed, spin the pedals backward a few more times, wait five minutes or so, and spin them backward again. This makes sure the lube is worked into all the little places it needs to be.

Now take a paper towel and hold it loosely around the chain and spin it back through again. You're doing this to wipe off the excess lube on the outside of the chain.

But, I hear you ask, didn't I just put that lube there for a reason? Yes and no. The part of the chain that is important to lubricate is the inside, in the pins, where the chain rubs and flexes as you pedal. That's where the lube needs to be. On the outside of your chain, a little oily lube is great because it'll keep the chain from rusting. But too much just acts like a dirt magnet and turns your chain into a great goopy mess that will wear out faster. So wipe off the excess loosely, leaving a light film to protect against rust.

If your bike has coaster brakes and you can't pedal backward, you have to do the same procedure while pedaling forward. To do that, have a friend lift the bike by the seat and hold the rear wheel off the ground. (You can also hook the seat on the edge of your kitchen table and do this alone if you have to. Put newspaper under the bike where you're dripping the lube if you're doing this inside.) Once the rear wheel is off the ground, you can pedal slowly forward to lube the chain. Be careful, though. The rear wheel will be spinning, and you do not want to get fingers, toes, or any other body part caught in the spokes.

How often do you have to lube your chain? It depends. If your bike is parked indoors and you don't ride that often, you can go months without having to worry. If it's parked outside, in the rain sometimes, or you ride it a lot, every month is a good idea. If it's squeaky or looks rusty, you're not lubing it enough.

TIRES AND TUBES

@%#! FLAT TIRES

If you ride any distance or any time at all, you're going to have a flat tire eventually. (Heck, you'll get a flat even if you don't ride at all and just let your bike sit. Like a balloon, bike tubes seep air at the molecular level and eventually go soft.)

AVOIDING FLATS

Let's start by trying to avoid flats. There are two ways. First, you can buy flat-proof tubes and have them installed in your tires. (Unlike car tires, most bicycle tires still need tubes inside them to hold the air. There are tubeless wheels and tires out there, but mostly for mountain bike racers.) Flat-proof tubes are either very thick rubber, or filled with sealant, or both. The thick flat-proof tubes are both heavier and tend to give a slightly harsher ride than regular tubes, but it's a reasonable trade-off if you get a lot of flats.

The second way to avoid a flat is to fill your current tubes with sealant, like Slime or Airlock. Unfortunately, this is not yet as easy as it should be, and it may be easier to buy new tubes already filled with sealant. (To fill your existing tubes, you have to pull the valve core out with a special tool that's included with the sealant, fill the tube with the goopy stuff, then reinstall the valve core and air up the tube. It's doable, but dumb.) A bike shop can do it for you in just a few minutes.

FIXING A FLAT

Fixing a flat is doable and not a bad skill to have. It's also something most bike shops will do for $5 or $10, so keep that in mind and choose accordingly.

If your rides take you away from town, it's a no-brainer to carry a spare tube, pump, and tire irons with you. Tubes and tire irons (and a patch kit) can get stuffed into a little storage pouch that attaches under your seat. Pumps get attached to the frame of your bike. If you don't have the stuff on your bike, you'll have to hoof it home and fix the flat there. Here's an overview, then step-by-step instructions. The method for getting the wheel off varies from bike to bike, and from front to back.

OVERVIEW

- Take the wheel off the bike.

- Pry one edge of the tire off the wheel so you can take the tube out.

- Take out the old tube out.

- Check the tire for thorns or nails (so you don't puncture your new tube too!)

- Install the new tube.

- Reseat the tire on the wheel and inflate the tube.

- Finally, reinstall the wheel on your bike and ride home.

Cross-country racers can do this in under two minutes, but they are weird people who get up early, drive long distances, and pay good money to suffer badly, so we won't worry much about them.

Here's how to remove the wheel. Start by taking a look at it. You need to see what kinds of brakes you have to deal with and how the wheel attaches to the bike. (Like your seat, it'll either be a quick release or nuts.) Start with the brakes. If you have coaster brakes, skip ahead because you don't need to mess with any stinkin' brakes. If you have brakes you apply by squeezing a lever, you may have to loosen them in order to get the wheel off the bike. How they loosen can vary.

If it's a fairly new mountain-type bike, the brake arms separate when you take the tip of the curvy piece at the end of the brake cable (technically called the "noodle") out of the slot it fits into on the other arm. Older-style cantilever brakes usually have a release lever on the brake itself or on the brake lever. Flip the lever, and you create enough slack to slip the wheel out. Bikes with skinny tires and wheels often don't have any release at all because you can slip the wheel in and out without loosening the brakes.

So, however it happens on your bike, step one is loosening the brakes if you need to.

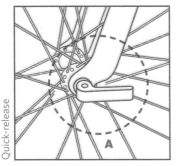

Quick-release

Now, take a look at the wheel itself. An axle runs through the center of the wheel and attaches the wheel to the bike. That attachment will either be a quick release—look for a lever—or nuts that thread onto each end of the axle. If it's nuts, get out your crescent wrenches again and take a look at the section on adjusting your seat (page 82) for tips on how to use them.

Before you loosen the attachment, lift the bike up by the handlebars, flip it over, and set it upside down on its seat and handlebars. Now, loosen the wheel attachment either by opening the quick release **(see figure A)** or loosening the nuts. If it's a quick release, the front wheel may not lift straight out even when you've opened it. They put little tabs on the front fork to keep wheels from coming off if the quick release gets accidentally opened while you ride. (There is no jaw-breaking face-plant that comes faster or harder than the front wheel suddenly coming off your bike while you ride.) To get the wheel off, hold the nut on the opposite side of the axle from the quick-release lever and spin the lever itself counter-clockwise. A few revolutions around and you'll be able to lift the wheel out.

Remember, you'll have to tighten the quick release the same amount when you reattach the wheel.

Front wheels lift straight out. Rear wheels lift out or forward and out. With the rear wheel, you also have to deal with the chain. Once the wheel is loose, hold the chain with your left hand and lift the wheel a little with your right. When the wheel is free of the bike, lift the chain off the toothed sprocket and pull the wheel out and to the side to clear the chain. You can just let the chain dangle there on the bike until you're ready to put the wheel back on.

Okay, now the wheel is off the bike. Let's get the tire off the wheel—or more accurately, let's get one side of the tire off the wheel. You don't need to take it completely off.

To get the tire off, you'll need at least two tire irons, small plastic pry bars that come with most tube-repair kits or are sold separately for a few nickels. Usually two will do the trick, but a third can come in handy if your tires are stubborn.

Tire Iron

To start, let out any air that's left in the tube. If you're being forced to change a flat, this has already been done for you. Next, take one tire iron and slip it between the tire and rim of the wheel on the far side of the wheel from the valve stem **(see illustration)**. Catch the edge of the tire with the tip of the tire iron, and pull the iron toward you and down to pry that edge of the tire out of the rim. Hook that tire iron under a spoke and leave it there, holding the tire. (If you can't hook it, you'll just have to hold it.) Now take your second tire iron and do the same thing four or five inches away from the first. Pry up that second part of the tire, which will pull up the length of the tire between the two tire irons. Usually, that's enough to loosen the whole tire, and all you have to do is slide a finger or a tire iron around between the side of the rim and the tire's edge and you'll loosen the rest. Sometimes, it takes prying up a third bit of tire with the third tire iron to get it to go. (And if you think this is hard and frustrating, try it with a damn motorcycle tire and wheel some time. I guarantee you'll work up a sweat, bloody a knuckle, and swear enough to make a sailor blush before you're done. At least my wife did . . .)

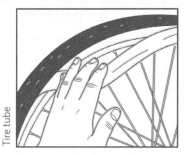

Tire tube

Now the tire should be out of the rim all the way around on one side. Reach in and pull the inner tube out **(see illustration)**. You'll have to push the valve stem down through the hole in the wheel to get it out, and a few valve stems have small nuts that hold them in place in the hole. Spin the nut off if you have to, then push the valve through and pull the tube completely out. You can patch it if you want, but new tubes are only a few bucks so we're going to skip the patching procedure. (If you're out on the road somewhere and don't have a spare and need to patch the tube, there will be instructions on the patch kit itself.)

Before you put in a new tube, reach inside the tire and rub your fingers all the way around it on the inside. You're feeling for a thorn or nail or piece of glass that's poking through on the inside that you may not be able to see from the outside. (You may well cut yourself doing this, so feel slowly.) If you find something, either push it out and take it out from the outside of the tire, or if that doesn't work, pull it through from the inside. Do whatever it takes to get rid of it. Few things are more frustrating than replacing a tube and immediately getting a new flat.

Now, take your new tube and pump a little air into it. You're not making life preservers or balloon animals here, just giving it enough air to hold its shape. Take the valve stem and line it up with the hole in the rim. Push the tube into the tire there, then work all the way around so the whole tube is inside the tire. (It's still off to the side of the rim at this point.) Now, work the valve stem through the hole and push the tube and tire over so they're centered over the rim. It'll look like the wheel is ready to go, except that the edge of the tire isn't tucked into the rim. So now we tuck it in.

Start by the valve stem, and push the edge of the tire inside the edge of the rim. You'll be able to do this with your fingers. Work your way around in both directions. Toward the end, the tire will feel tight and it'll be hard to slide the edge over the rim. At that point, use your tire irons again to pry the tire back into place. It's usually not too hard. When the tire slips into place, look at the valve stem. It should be sticking straight up through the rim. If it's angled over, slide the tire and tube around on the rim slightly until it's right. Then pump up the tube.

Reattach the wheel to your bike. If it's a rear wheel, make sure to put the chain back on the sprocket. Also make sure the wheel is lined up straight with your bike—it's possible to slip it in at an angle if you're not paying attention. Tighten the wheel, either with the axle nuts or by closing the quick-release. (It should take a fair amount of pressure to close the quick-release lever. If there's no pressure, it's not holding your wheel on at all, so open the lever, tighten it by spinning it clockwise, then lock it down again. It's a trial-and-error process to find the right pressure.)

Attaching the brakes

When the wheel is back on, flip the bike back over, reattach your brakes if necessary **(see illustration)**, and take it for a test ride. Brakes that rub now (and didn't before) are a sigh that the wheel isn't in straight. Loosen it again, straighten up the wheel, and retighten. (Quick releases are so handy it's not even funny.)

That's all it really takes, and it sounds harder than it is. If you're not sure you can remember all the steps to changing the tire, you could always practice in your living room some Sunday afternoon. Just pretend you have a flat tire and walk through taking the wheel off and taking the tube out. Then put it all back together and try your bike out. Once you've done it once, it'll be easy the next time.

LOCK IT
OR LOSE IT

MINE, MINE, MINE!

One last word about bikes. If you like your bike, lock it. Even if you don't like your bike but just don't want to spend the time and money to buy a new one, lock it. Lock it every time, unless it's inside your room. My daughter thought hers was safe because she put it on her porch, which was maybe three steps from the parking lot of her apartment complex. Her thinking—and I use that term loosely—was that since people aren't supposed to come onto your porch, her bike would be okay. Didn't work out that way. Turns out the people who will steal your bike don't mind a little trespassing to do it.

There are a bunch of different locks, and some are better than others, but it really doesn't matter in most cases. Any lock will work, because what the thieves are looking for is a bike that isn't locked at all, If you do have quick-release wheels, it's worth getting a cable lock that threads through both of them so you don't come out of class one day and find that you still have a bike, but it has no wheels. (Ease of theft is the only downside to quick releases.) There are also U-shaped locks, handcuff-shaped locks, and combo-style locks that combine a U-shaped lock with a cable.

Whatever type you get, just make sure to use it.

CHAPTER 4:

APARTMENTS

Here's the deal with apartments and other rentals: Yes, you have a landlord you can call to take care of problems in your unit. But some landlords are slow to fix minor problems, and there may be some problems you don't want your landlord to know about. There are also safety issues that are best for you to take care of yourself, regardless of what the landlord wants or does. This chapter will cover some of those basic around-the-place kinds of things that may crop up that you can handle. Some of these hold true for dorms, too, but you usually have less opportunity and need to deal with repair issues in dorms.

Beyond these things, if something goes wrong at your apartment or rental, call in the landlord. Having someone else on the hook when the water heater craps out is one of the benefits of being a renter.

LOCKS AND SECURITY

KEEP OUT!

We'll start at the front door, specifically the lock. For safety, you want there to be a deadbolt on every exterior door, not just the lock on the knob. If the apartment you're looking at doesn't have deadbolts, ask to have them installed or consider looking elsewhere. Deadbolts won't keep out a determined thief, but nothing will. What a deadbolt and a few other common-sense security measures will do is keep out an opportunistic thief, and that's nine-tenths of the battle.

RE-KEYING OR REPLACING LOCKS

Some people re-key the locks when they rent a new place, so old tenants who may have kept or copied a key can't break in. (Most apartment complexes and rentals don't allow this, however, so if you do it, do it quietly.) It's easy, too. Most deadbolts can be removed by taking out two screws on the lock and two on the faceplate, and a deadbolt the same make and size will slip right in. You can even save the old one and reinstall it when you move out, so your landlord will never even know you replaced the deadbolt.

There's a danger with this, of course. If you ever need your landlord to come over and do any work, you'll have to be there or he'll find out you've replaced the lock. And if there's an emergency when you're not home—a water leak for instance—and the landlord can't get in, expect him to bill you for absolutely everything that got damaged.

OTHER LOCK (AND LIQUOR) ISSUES

As mentioned in the introduction, if your locks are gummed up and sticky, squirt a little WD-40 in the slot and slide your key in and out a few times.

What about when your key goes in, but the door doesn't unlock? I know it sounds stupid, but are you sure you're at the right door? Every year a few folks, most of them really drunk, think they're home but their keys don't work, and they get themselves shot trying to break into a house or apartment they only thought was theirs. (Don't get that drunk. Bad things happen when you're that drunk.) If you are at the right place—and using the right key—and the door doesn't unlock, you'll have to call your landlord. The lock needs fixing or replacing, and they are required to do it.

WINDOWS AND SLIDING GLASS DOORS

Your windows and sliding glass doors should also lock, and if the locking mechanism is damaged, get them fixed. Some people who live on upstairs floors figure it's not important to get the locks on their sliding glass doors fixed. What they don't realize is that there are people who make a living breaking into upstairs apartments.

If your windows slide open and closed, you can buy little thumbscrew locks you attach to the frame. What they do is let you open your windows only a little, but keep them from being pushed all the way open. If you want a little ventilation but don't want to leave the window all the way open, they're the ticket. The problem is that if your window slides open far enough to offer any decent ventilation, it's also open for enough for someone to get their fingers inside and lift the window out of its frame. So don't rely on them too much. Broom handles or sticks set in the tracks of sliding glass doors or sliding windows work on the same principle.

LOW-COST ALARMS

Alarms are an option, but not a common one in most apartment complexes or rentals. There are portable alarms marketed to frequent travelers to use in hotel rooms, which hook over your doorknob and shriek if someone opens the door.

In a duplex or rental house, there's another option. A trick a lot of cops use is to buy decals and a dummy alarm box from a local security company. I did it once at a rental where I lived, and it cost me $20. Screw the empty box above the garage where it's nice and visible, and slap a few stickers on the main windows. Most thieves won't chance it. There are too many places out there without alarms to risk hitting a place that might have one. (I suppose you could steal one of those yard signs people have that say, "These premises monitored by So and So Alarm Company," and while that would be ironic and amusing, it would also be morally wrong. Possibly more amusing than wrong, but that's for you to decide.)

SAFETY VS. CONVENIENCE

All home security stuff comes down to a balance between safety and convenience. You can lock every door and window all the time—even when you take out the garbage—install alarms and do everything right from a security standpoint but never hear the breeze through the trees at night again. And for certain people and in certain places, this is absolutely the right and responsible thing to do.

Or you can leave your doors and windows open and come and go as you please, knowing that thieves and bad guys can, too. There's no right answer here. You have to do what is right for you, but be smart at the same time. You don't want uninvited people in your apartment, and you can't count on your neighbors to spot a stranger. Apartment complexes are big anonymous places, and people who don't belong there look just like the people who do. If you live somewhere that allows pets, the absolute best home security system you can have is a territorial dog.

Nobody messes with a territorial dog.

ELECTRICAL STUFF

WHAT A SHOCK

Electricity scares me. It does. I've tried to learn about it and understand the physics behind it, but my brain just can't wrap itself around electron streams making motors work. As far as I'm concerned, electricity is some sort of magic, and like all magic, it's just a little scary. So don't expect instructions on how to rewire a lamp (which isn't all that hard) or rewind an electric motor (which is). We're going to stay a little more basic, like how to turn the power to your place on and off.

Let's say you're boiling an egg, doing a load of dishes, and go into the bathroom to dry your hair. You turn on the hair dryer and bam!—all the lights go out.

Pretty common, actually.

You've blown a breaker (or a fuse, if your place is really old), and you'll need to reset the breaker (or replace the fuse) to get your power back.

CIRCUITS AND BREAKERS

Circuit breakers are built into every house and apartment to keep them from burning down. If you overload an electrical circuit, it heats up. Heat it up enough, and the insulation melts off. When that hot, un-insulated wire touches something, it can easily start a fire, and your house is toast.

Breakers keep electric circuits from getting overloaded. Your place will have several separate circuits—one for all the overhead lights, one for all the wall outlets, one for the stove, one for the dryer, etc. Each will have a separate breaker, which is designed to trip—and cut the power to that circuit—if it senses an overload.

In addition to those individual breakers, there will be one more—the main. The main circuit breaker cuts power to all the others when it trips—leaving your whole place dark.

If you blow an individual breaker, it means you've overloaded that circuit. You've plugged too many things into that line or you're trying to run an appliance that draws too much juice. (I used to blow fuses in my old garage if I used the shop vac and air compressor at the same time.) Try to figure out what is causing the overload before you reset the breaker. (If you don't, it'll just trip again.) My sister has an old house, and she can't vacuum and wash or dry clothes at the same time, and if her husband is using any of his power tools, turning on an extra light is dicey. They've learned what they can and can't do at the same time and live with it.

BREAKER BOX

Because everything went dark, you can figure you blew your main breaker. (Things that heat up—like electric stoves, dishwashers, and hair dryers—typically put a bigger strain on a circuit than things that don't.) What you need to do now is make your way to your breaker box. It's usually in an out-of-the-way but still accessible location. In an apartment, it'll be inside the unit somewhere. In a utility room, an attached garage, or sometimes in a back hallway. It'll look like a small metal door about a foot wide and a foot and a half or so tall built into the wall at chest height.

In a house or duplex, it'll typically be outside and looks like a shallow metal box screwed to your wall. It could be in a basement or utility room. When you've found it, open it.

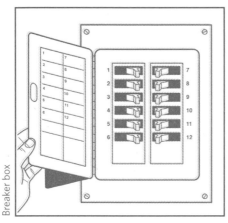

Breaker box

If it's a breaker box, you'll see rows of switches (see illustration). They look like light switches that toggle side to side. Fuse boxes, which are only in older homes and buildings, have round glass things that look like very small and heavy light bulbs—they're the fuses—screwed into receptacles. Breakers are easier.

When a circuit breaker trips, the switch itself loosens. It may not flip all the way to the "off" position, but it's no longer set in to "on" either. What you need to do is find the right breaker and toggle it off and then back on.

How do you find the right breaker? Hopefully, they're labeled (and you own a flashlight if it's dark). If not, it's trial and error. Flip them all off one by one, then back to the on position. Usually, you'll be able to feel the tripped breaker because it'll flip to "off" easier than the others. When you get the right one, whatever circuit went off will come back to life. If it was the main, all the lights and everything else will come back on. That includes the stove burner you had on originally, so unless you want your hard-boiled eggs to explode (which happens if you boil all the water off and leave them on the burner too long), make sure to turn stuff off.

If you have fuses, shine your flashlight on each one. Inside the glass fuse you'll see a metal strip. If the fuse is good, you'll see a solid strip. When a fuse blows, that strip melts, and you'll see a gap (and often a little smoke on the glass). Unscrew the fuse, and replace it with one exactly the same. The fuse will be labeled—15 amps, 20 amps, something like that. Make sure to put the same type of fuse back in. Some people who aren't as smart as they think they are put a bigger fuse in "so they won't blow it again," replacing a 20-amp fuse with a 30. And while that may keep the fuse from blowing, it may also burn your duplex down. Breakers and fuses are protecting you when they blow. I know it's annoying, but be thankful they did.

EMERGENCY! CUT!
Let's say you're about to vacuum, and you plug your vacuum in and the outlet starts sparking and smoking and doing all kinds of stuff that looks like electricity gone bad. In this case, you want to yank the cord out and then throw the

breakers as soon as you can. Same is true if it's your air conditioner or electric stove or water heater that's acting up. The idea is that cutting off the power at the breaker will stop the flow of electricity to the problem outlet or appliance and prevent a fire. (If a fire has already started, cutting off the power won't stop it. A fire extinguisher or the local fire department needs to do that.)

If you need to cut power to a circuit in your house, just push the breaker switch to off. If your breakers aren't labeled and it's an emergency, flip the main off or just flip all of them off. (If your breakers aren't labeled, there's no law that says you can't be the one to do it. Go through them one at a time on some Sunday when you're bored, and write what they control next to each switch.)

Beyond that, if anything electrical goes wrong, call the landlord.

PLUMBING

JUST SAY NO TO CRACK

Plumbing is another thing that it's good to know a little about, but you should call your landlord if there are any big problems.

We'll cover just a few basics: fixing a stopped-up toilet, fixing a toilet that won't flush (or stop flushing), getting a slow-draining sink or shower to work, retrieving a ring or other valuable item dropped down a sink, and changing a shower head. All of these are things you can do yourself.

THE TOILET
TAKING THE PLUNGE
The most immediate of all plumbing problems happens when you flush and the poo doesn't. Your toilet backs up, and instead of going down, the water (and the rest) rises up. Fortunately, even if the toilet is completely blocked, one flush usually won't overflow and spill out onto your floor. What you'll need to do is let the water stop rising and get out your trusty plunger. Don't have a plunger? Put it on

your shopping list and buy one the next time you're out. They are one of those things you don't need often, but when you do nothing else will work.

Believe it or not, there are different kinds of plungers, and some work better than others. The good ones have a kind of bulb-shaped business end that fits into the bottom of a toilet bowl. These work better than the standard old-school dome-shaped ones, but are a bit more expensive. Whatever kind you get, they're all pretty easy to use.

1. Put your plunger into the toilet and position it over the hole where the water is supposed to drain out.

2. Now, slowly at first, push—plunge—it down. The idea is that you're pushing water against the blockage, and that the water pressure will force it free. (It's the same principle that makes the brakes work in your car, by the way—see page 40 for more on brakes.) Go slowly at first because you'll have air trapped in your plunger during that first push, and you don't want to make big splashing bubbles.

3. Once the air is out, plunge away, down and up as many times as it takes to clear away the blockage. You're trying for a tight seal and well-directed pressure here, not speed. You'll know you've cleared it when the toilet drains. (Until the toilet drains, be real careful about flushing again so you don't cause an overflow.)

4. If after much plunging the toilet is still stopped up, call your landlord and have him or her them send a plumber.

OTHER FLUSHING FIXES
There are two other flushing-related problems you may encounter: Pushing the flush handle and nothing happens, or pushing the handle and having the toilet flush but not stop flushing. These are both easy problems to fix.

WHEN IT WON'T FLUSH
If you push the handle and nothing at all happens, what's probably happened is that the chain that connects the handle to the flapper inside your toilet tank has come off. (The piece really is called a flapper, too.) To fix it, you'll have to take the top off the toilet tank and reattach the chain.

The tank is that square boxy part above the toilet bowl, and the lid just lifts off. Remove the lid and set it aside. Take a look inside. Starting at the top, find the flush handle. (What you see from the outside of the toilet is just half of it.) The whole handle is like a see-saw—when you press down on the outside half, the inside half goes up. It's connected to the flapper at the very bottom of the toilet tank by a metal or plastic chain, and when the handle goes up, it lifts the flapper. When the flapper goes up, the weight of the water in the tank forces the water in the toilet bowl down, flushing it. When the tank is empty, the flapper falls back down and the tank refills. It's a really simple and effective system.

So if you press the handle and the toilet doesn't flush, chances are the chain has come off or broken. Usually you'll see it sitting down at the bottom of the tank. To fix it, all you have to do is reach in, lift the chain up, and reconnect it to the inner arm of the handle. If the chain is broken, which sometimes happens when they're old and rusty, you can usually use a paper clip to connect the two ends and it'll work fine.

But isn't the water in the tank all toilety and gross? Actually, it's not. The water in the tank has come straight from your pipes. It's never been in the toilet bowl (and won't ever be if you don't get the chain fixed)! Toilet tanks can be rusty or a little slimy, but there's no poo or pee in them to worry about, so you can reach in and fix what needs fixing without shoulder-length rubber gloves. (It is always a good idea to wash your hands afterward, though.)

Once the chain is reconnected to the flapper and handle, test it. Flush and watch what happens inside the tank. The flapper should go up and stay up while the water drains out of the tank, then fall down and seal completely. If the chain is too long, the flapper may not rise up enough to stay up by itself and let the water flow out. If that's the case, adjust your paper clip or the connection to the handle to shorten the chain.

WHEN IT WON'T STOP FLUSHING

If your toilet runs all the time, it's because the flapper isn't sealing completely. If that's the case, check to see if the chain is too short or got caught on something and is being held open. Adjust it so the flapper can close completely. If the chain has slack in it and the flapper still doesn't seal, make sure there isn't an extra length of chain or anything else beneath the flapper holding it open. If there's nothing blocking the flapper that you can see but your toilet still runs all the time, call your landlord. A running toilet wastes hundreds of gallons of water a day.

SLOW DRAINS, SINKS, AND SHOWERS

One time when my wife was visiting our daughter down in Santa Barbara she took a shower and found herself standing in ankle-deep soapy water the whole time. Afterward, she asked Gina how long it'd been like that.

"About a month," Gina answered.

"Have you tried Drano?" my wife asked.

"What's Drano?" our 3.85-GPA-science-student daughter replied. (She could be your child's pediatrician someday, so don't laugh.)

Drano is a product that dissolves away clogs in sink and shower drains. It's a very caustic chemical—you don't want to get any on you or your clothes—but it works great for clearing clogged and slow-running sinks if you can't clear the blockage yourself. (Liquid Plumber is another good brand. There are others as well.)

The first thing to do is see if you can pull up all the hair and goop that's stopping up your sink and shower with your fingers or needle-nosed pliers. (See page 221 for more on pliers.) Often times, this is all it takes.

If not, and you want to take chemical action, get some drain opener at the local store.

The thick, gel-like liquids work the best, and all you have to do is pour the recommended amount into your sink or shower, let it sit for 15 minutes or so, then run lots of hot water down the drain. If it doesn't work the first time, try a second time. It'll usually do the trick. (It worked on the first try at my daughter's place.) If it still doesn't work, call the landlord.

RETRIEVING STUFF
DROPPED DOWN THE SINK

Here's an unhappy moment: You're getting undressed after a night on the town and drop a diamond earring into your sink. Or a cufflink. (Does anybody still wear cufflinks?) You grab for it, but before you can reach it that quarter-carat disappears down the drain.

It happens. Fortunately, you can get your earring back 99 percent of the time, as long as you do not run the water. And believe it or not, you have sewer gases to thank.

Take a look under your sink. You'll see a pipe coming down straight from the drain. It attaches to a J-shaped piece of pipe that attaches to more pipes that disappear into the wall.

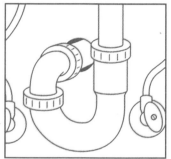

Sink trap

It's that J-shaped piece of pipe that's important here. It's called a trap, and even though it's there to keep sewer gases out of your bathroom, it'll also let you retrieve a lost doodad. You may need a few tools for this, but it's doable. (And in case you care how it keeps sewer gases out, it's like this: The J of the trap stays filled with a little bit of water all the time, and that water acts as a plug keeping the stinky gasses in the sewer lines where they belong. Sometimes in a house that's been sitting empty a long time, you'll smell a sewery smell from the sinks because the water in the traps evaporated away. Just run a little water down the sink, and it'll be fine again.)

OPENING A SINK TRAP:

HERE'S WHAT YOU'LL NEED: BUCKET OR PAN (TO CATCH TRAPPED WATER), A PAIR OF LARGE CHANNEL-LOCK PLIERS OR A PIPE WRENCH, AND TEFLON TAPE.

1. Now don't freak out. Channel-lock pliers are just big adjustable pliers that can grab skinny stuff or wide stuff. Drain pipes are fairly wide, so you need a pair of channel-locks big enough to get a good grip on your pipes. (The jaws of the pliers should be on opposite sides of the pipe. If they're not, the pliers aren't big enough.) Pipe wrenches are just big adjustable wrenches made for plumbing work. You can get either at a local hardware store. Teflon tape sounds all high-tech, but it's just a thin strip of white plasticy Teflon sold in a roll that looks like first-aid tape. It's not even sticky, and it's less than a buck at any hardware store. And if the pipes are plastic, you probably won't need any of it.

2. Okay, here's what you're gonna do. Put the bucket under the sink trap and get down there yourself so you can see. At either end of the trap, you're going to find a nut that holds the trap in place. What you need to do is loosen both of those nuts. If the pipes are plastic, you'll probably be able to do it with your hands. If they're metal, you'll likely need to use the wrench or pliers. Get a good tight grip on the nut and turn it counter-clockwise. (Lefty-loosy, righty-tighty.) Loosen both all the way, and the trap will pull straight down. (The nuts don't come off in your hands—they stay attached to the bits of pipe under the sink.) You may need to wiggle the trap a little to get it free. When it comes off, water—and your diamond earring—will pour out into the bucket. Yeah!

If there's also a lot of gunk in there, now's a good time to clean it out. Once it's clean, you'll need to reattach the trap.

3 . Start by pushing it back in place. Twist the nuts onto the threads in the trap, and then tighten them moderately tight. (Don't go crazy. They idea isn't to have the tightest nuts on the block, just to have them snug enough so the drain doesn't leak.) So tighten them and test it—run water in the sink and let it drain. Let it run for a minute at full power. If there are no leaks, no drips, no water drops forming on the underside of the pipe, it's good and you're done.

If there are leaks, try tightening the nuts a bit more. If that doesn't work—and especially if your pipes are metal—you'll want to try some Teflon tape. Take the trap off again and wrap Teflon tape tightly around both threaded ends. Try to get a nice flat band around the treads, but don't worry if it bunches up here or there. Put a couple of wraps around the threads. When you tighten the nut down onto those threads, the Teflon will keep water from leaking through the joint.

If there are still leaks, call your landlord and tell him or her your sink is leaking. You could say you took the trap off to get a lost earring, but you can also keep that fact to yourself and just imply you're a very conscientious renter looking out for the property.

REPLACING A SHOWER HEAD

I hear you asking: why would I want to replace the shower head? Maybe you just don't like it. Maybe it's getting all calcified and only shoots two streams of water. Maybe it's one of those adjustable shower massage deals and the dial has broken. If it happens, this is a repair you can handle cheaply and quickly.

First, buy a new shower head. Figure on spending $10 to $40. (If yours is broken, send in the receipt with your next rent check and ask for a refund.) If you don't have Teflon tape, get some now. (It's described in the sinks section, page 118.) Other than that, you'll need a small crescent wrench. That's it.

Use the wrench to spin off the old shower head. It shouldn't be too hard. Wrap Teflon tape around the threaded end of the pipe sticking out of the wall. Spin on the new shower head, tightening it down just enough so it doesn't leak.

Done. Took all of five minutes. Enjoy the shower.

WALLS

LET'S HANG SOMETIME

There are two basic things you might want to do to walls: Hang stuff on them, and destroy all evidence of having hung stuff on them.

HANGING STUFF ON YOUR WALLS

Light stuff is easy. Thumbtacks and finish nails—small nails with itsy-bitsy heads at the top (see figure 1, next page)—can be pushed or tapped in just about anywhere. Screws (see figure 2) hold better than nails, but both work for really light things.

The trick is hanging heavy stuff—that big wood-framed mirror for instance. For that, you're gonna need to find a stud. (Even if you are one, tough guy . . .)

The studs we're talking about here are the 2-by-4 pieces of lumber inside your walls. The wall you see is probably made of gypsum wallboard that is attached to these 2-by-4 studs. Studs are placed every 16 inches in most cases, so

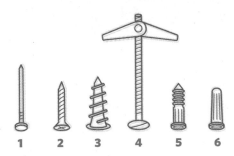

1   **2**   **3**   **4**   **5**   **6**

there should be one at least near where you want to hang your heavy mirror. You need to find a stud because heavy objects—things weighing more than 20 pounds or so—will just pull a nail or screw right out of the soft wallboard if you don't take precautions. The easiest precaution is hanging stuff that heavy on a screw driven through the wallboard into the solid wood stud behind it. Here's how.

1 . You'll need a stud sensor. (I swear I'm not making this up.) They sell them at Target and K-mart and the like and at all hardware stores. They are small battery-operated devices a little bigger than a deck of cards that sense the density of the wall and tell where the high-density spots are. Those high-density spots are studs. You set the sensor against the wall, activate it, then slide it slowly along the wall horizontally. With lights or a beep—they vary brand to brand—it'll tell you when you've found the edges of a stud, and some even tell you when you've found the center of one. Make marks with a pencil at both edges. (And don't be surprised that those marks will only be an inch-and-a-half apart. 2-by-4 lumber is really 3½-by-1½ lumber. Go figure.)

2 . Drive a screw in the middle of the stud at whatever height you want, and it'll hold most anything. (Studs run straight up and down, floor to ceiling.)

It's sometimes possible to just tap your way along a wall and listen, using the difference in sound to try figure out where a stud is. It does occasionally work, but usually results in two or three extra holes in your wall.

3 . The easiest screws to use are Phillips-head drywall screws **(see figure 3)**. The +-shaped head and wide, sharp threads make them easy to drive and very strong. You'll want 1½-inch to 2-inch long screws for hanging stuff.

WHAT IF YOU ABSOLUTELY HAVE TO HANG SOMETHING WHERE THERE'S NO STUD?
Get used to disappointment.

Seriously, there are ways to do it, and I'll tell you about a couple of them. But it's an apartment and it's not an easy thing to hide and there will be a stud within eight inches in one direction or the other. Are you sure your heavy-ass wall décor has to go right here?

I know, I know. It has to be here.

HANGING ON WALL BOARD

To hang something heavy on just wallboard, you need to use an anchor or molly bolt **(see figure 4)**. There are a few variants on the theme, but basically what they do is hold the wallboard from both the front and back, so it spreads out the load and pressure over a wider area, allowing you to hang heavier items.

Molly bolts are thin bolts inside a tubular metal wrapping. You drill a hole in the wall the size of the outside of the wrapping and push the bolt in place. The front has a wide flat head that sits flush against the wall. With a screwdriver, start turning the bolt. The back end of the wrapping is threaded, and as you turn the bolt, it pulls the wrapping forward toward the wall. As it mushrooms and deforms, it makes a nice strong metal stop against the back of the wallboard. The problem is getting mollies out. There isn't any way to that doesn't leave pretty big holes in the wall, and landlords universally object to big holes in the wall.

OTHER WALL ANCHORS

There are other wall anchors **(see figures 5 and 6, page 122)**. One style has a sharp pointed end and oversized screw threads. You set them on a screwdriver, shove the sharp end of the anchor into the wall so it pierces the wallboard, then screw in the oversize threads until the front face is flush with the wall. You then screw a regular screw into the hole where the screwdriver went. They work for medium-heavy stuff, but you have to be careful you don't shove the whole dang thing through the wall when you first try to get it started. It leaves a hole in your wall about the size of a nickel. (And yes, as a matter of fact, I do have first-hand experience with this, thanks for asking...) Taking these out of the wall when you move is easier than removing a molly bolt, but they still leave a decent-sized hole you'll have to patch.

Okay, let's say I've convinced you that heavy-duty anchors aren't a good idea for hanging something between studs in an apartment, but you still want to hang your mirror where there's no stud. There is a way. What you can do is drive screws on the two nearest studs and string a length of wire between them. You can hang your mirror from the wire, and as long as it's wide enough to cover the screws, no one will know you cheated. And the screw holes you made will be much easier to patch than the alternatives when you move out.

PATCHING HOLES

If you've made a bunch of holes in your walls, you'll eventually have to patch them. Fortunately, most apartments are basic white, and small repairs are pretty invisible even without hiding them with paint. (If your walls are blue, white spackling compound will only call attention to itself.)

It's easiest if the holes you need to patch are small: tack and nail holes and assorted screw holes. Larger nickel- to quarter-size holes are harder to repair and a lot harder to hide.

1 . You'll need two things from your local hardware store: A small plastic putty knife and a small tub of spackling compound. The putty knife isn't a knife at all. In fact, it looks more like a frosting spatula—a flat, flexible blade with a handle—and it works just like a frosting spatula. (What the heck, if you've got a frosting spatula, you can certainly use that.) The spackling compound is a white putty. (They make some now that's purple when you put it on but turns white as it dries. If you like color, knock yourself out.)

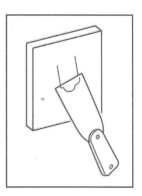

2 . Patching small holes is very easy. Dip a corner of the putty knife in the spackle to pick up just a little and then press it against the wall, using pressure to force the spackle into the hole. You want to put as little spackle as possible on the wall; use the blade to press it thin and flat. The idea is to fill the hole and not have the spackle make a big, noticeable smooth spot around it. Walls are textured—it hides imperfections—and too much spackle will show. So just use a little. If there's too much, wet an old washcloth so it's damp and rub the excess away.

SMALL HOLES

Small tack, nail, and most screw holes can be done with one application, but larger holes will need two or more coats. Spackle shrinks as it dries, so a large repair may dimple or crack, and it'll take a second shot the next day to finish it off. Follow the same principles outlined above—use as little compound as possible and keep it in the hole and not on the wall.

If your repairs are small and subtle, they'll be next to invisible even if the white of the spackle isn't exactly the same color white as your paint. If you have access to the paint that was used on your walls, you can dab a little over the repairs to further hide them.

LARGER HOLES

If the hole was the size of a nickel and now you have a smooth spot where you filled it in, you can use a little more spackle to texture over the repair. Put a little on your putty knife, then try to make it blend with the wall around it. Sometimes you'll lift the knife to give it little dimples, sometimes you'll spread it like frosting. Do whatever most matches the wall around it. If you get it close, no one will ever know. If it's a big repair—your not-supposed-to-be-there terrier decided to eat a wall one day—you may need to buy a can of spray-on texture, sold at hardware stores. They shoot out the same kind of texturing compound that was originally sprayed onto your walls when the apartment was built. You'll pretty much have to paint to hide this repair, so try not to let your puppy eat your walls.

CANDLES ON CARPET

BURNING LOVE

I speak for parents everywhere when I say if you've had candles in your bedroom and spilled wax on the carpet, we don't want to know. We don't want to know when or how or especially why (or with whom). Here's how to save the carpet so we never find out.

Start by scraping up whatever wax you can with an old butter knife. This is the one-and-only household repair where an old butter knife is actually the correct tool.

When you've gotten all you reasonably can (and it's much easier on flat carpets than shaggy ones) get out your steam iron and a sacrificial bath towel. This procedure will ruin the towel, so if you don't have one you can spare, get one at a thrift store for a quarter. If you don't have an iron, they sell those at thrift stores, too.

Turn your iron to its highest steam setting and let it warm up. Put the towel over the wax, then set the iron on the towel, gently moving it around. The heat and steam will melt the wax, and the bath towel will soak it up. Heat it and check often, moving to clean spots on the towel until the wax is all out of the carpet.

CHAPTER 5:

MOVING

Moving is a pain in the butt, there are just no two ways about it. There's the sorting and the packing and the hauling and the cleaning—and that's just getting out. But there are a few tricks that make moving easier, and I've moved enough—and helped enough other people move—that I've learned a bunch of them. Hope these help.

SORTING

BUT IT'S MY FAVORITE SLEEP SHIRT!

The absolutely easiest things to pack, lift, carry, haul, unpack, and put away are the things you don't bring. Seriously. If you want to make your move as easy as possible, sort your stuff hard. The more you don't bring, the easier it will be.

I know this is easier said than done. I also used to think it was easier for guys than gals, until my son—who has more clothes, shoes, and musical instruments than many philharmonic orchestras—proved me wrong. But it's the key to making your move easier, so start looking at every single thing you own and ask yourself why.

Start with things that are stupid-heavy and easy to replace. If your shelves are planks sitting on concrete blocks, it may be a lot easier to replace the blocks on the other end than move the ones you have. Books are also ridiculously heavy. If there are books you're pretty sure you're not going to read or need again, now is the time to get rid of them.

I don't want to sound callous here, but gifts can go, too. I know someone gave you this thing and it has meaning and sentimental value, but really, did they expect you to keep it forever? The meaning and value in a gift comes from the giving, not the thing. You don't have to keep the stuff forever.

Also think about the space you're moving into. If you've got an eight-foot couch and the new apartment has a seven-foot wall, ditch the couch and replace it when you get moved in. If the new place has a built-in microwave, sell your freestanding one. If you have trouble letting go of things, here are some entirely arbitrary but remarkably effective rules that can help.

THE TWO-YEAR RULE
This one's easy: If you haven't used something in two years, you don't need it. It's that simple.

Those old jeans you want to fit into again one day? Gone. The crock pot Aunt Jennie gave you? Toast. Your third-grade schoolwork? History.

There are exceptions. Keep all the coursework in your major. (The rest of it, once grades are posted and official, is just a fire hazard.) Keep all your financial aid records. Keep tax returns pretty much forever, and all other tax-related documents for at least three years. Keep mementoes that are truly meaningful, and toss the ones that truly aren't.

Beyond that, it doesn't matter how expensive, tasteful, unique, or special something was when you got it, if you haven't used it in the past two years it's time to let it go.

And let me say this on behalf of parents everywhere: We love you and we support you, but we don't want your third-grade schoolwork either. Don't ditch it on us.

ALL YOU CAN CARRY

This is also called the one-trip method (or two-trip method, if you must . . .) And it's just that—whatever you can carry in one trip in whatever vehicle you own. I moved this way a half-dozen times, including once when I owned a 1964 VW Bug and once when I had a 1970 Plymouth Duster. (I'm not that old. The cars were already old when I bought them!)

I did make the two-trip exception once, when the vehicle I owned at the time was a 400cc Honda motorcycle. I also had a big, ugly, baby-blue Samsonite suitcase, which is not an easy thing to carry on a motorcycle. The only thing I could think to do was fill it up, set it behind me on the seat of the bike, then wrap duct tape around myself and the suitcase. I rode across Delaware to my new apartment with the suitcase taped to my back. After I unloaded it, I re-taped the empty suitcase to myself and rode back across the state, then loaded it up again and repeated the process. I have no idea how many Delaware traffic laws I violated, but it worked.

The only problem with the one-trip method is that unless you know how much you can fit in your Honda Accord, it's hard to know how much to get rid of before the day of your move. And you want to know what you'll be able to get rid of ahead of time to take advantage of the only upside to moving—the chance to cash in on the junk you're not taking with you.

MAKING IT PAY

If there is a silver lining to the hard sorting you're doing before a move it's that you may be able to pay for the whole move—or at least offset some of the expense—by selling stuff you're not taking.

The weekend before you move out, have a yard sale. Price everything to sell, and take what doesn't to Goodwill. Craigslist.com is great for that old sofa or bookcase. If you make $20 for it, fantastic. It's gravy. (In pre-Craigslist days we just put stuff out on the street with a "Free to Good Home" sign on it.) Many papers have free or discounted want ads for stuff worth less than $400 or $500, so that's worth considering, and the ad rates in the Thrifty Nickel–type free shoppers are low. Used bookstores pay cash; used record stores buy CDs and DVDs—you get the picture.

If you've got time before a move, you could list stuff on eBay, although I'm not sure I'd recommend it. Moving is a hectic time, and things get lost and forgotten and broken, and it may not be worth risking negative feedback from an unhappy buyer to get a few extra dollars in value for something.

PACKING

SURE IT'LL FIT!

Remember the super-continent Pangaea? That compact mass of continents before they all drifted apart and raised our long-distance rates?

Good packing is like reassembling Pangaea. Whether it's an individual box, your backseat, or a U-Haul, you want to fill in the empty spaces and have everything pressed together firmly. It may be counterintuitive, but things packed tightly together are safer than things packed loosely. When things are packed loosely, they slide and bounce and smash against one another. When they're packed tight, everything moves together (if it moves at all) and arrives at your new place safe.

WHY PANTIES ARE
BETTER THAN PEANUTS
(AND BOXERS ARE BETTER THAN BUBBLE WRAP)

When you pack, you're going to want to wrap at least a few breakables in some kind of padding to keep them safe. Some people use newspaper—messy and not very effective anyway—and some people buy plate protectors, bubble wrap, or Styrofoam peanuts.

Not only are those folks going to extra expense (and doing the planet no favors), they're overlooking all the natural packing pads they need to move and already own. Look in your sock drawer. There has never been better packing material created than socks, T-shirts, towels, and all the other clothes you have to move anyway.

Have plates you want to protect? Slip each one inside a T-shirt. Coffee cups? Stuff socks inside them, then wrap a washcloth or dishtowel outside them. Personally I see nothing wrong with using clean underwear for these tasks as well, but I know some people will think that's gross. (But I bet those people wash their underwear in the same laundry load as their dishtowels, so what's the difference?) Once it's wrapped, pack it tightly in a box. Tight is safe. If stuff can move around, it'll break. If it's all snug enough that nothing inside the box can shift, it's perfect. Mark the box "Fragile" and set it aside.

There's no need to wrap pots and pans or other stuff that doesn't break, although if you can fill the corners of the box with spatulas or paperbacks or anything else, so much the better.

HAVE A PLAN

It doesn't have to be a detailed plan or even a great plan. All your plan needs to do is help you stay out of your own way and not move anything more than once.

Here's what I mean. Let's say you box up your books, your pots and pans, and your dishes. If you stack them in your living room the way you'll want them stacked in a moving truck—heaviest stuff on bottom, fragile stuff on top—you end up having to move your dishes twice. (You'll move them off the heavy stuff so you can load the heavy boxes first.) Instead, put all the fragile stuff together in one corner. Keep the heavy stuff together in a different corner. Put it all toward the back of your room or your apartment so it's not in the way as you carry stuff out.

Other things to keep in mind: Don't pack a box heavier than you can carry. If a full box of books is too much, fill the bottom with books and the top with sweaters. Or cereal.

(Don't get hung up on keeping stuff separated by room—it's all got to get unpacked and put into brand new places, anyway.) If you've got a ton of boxes, number them. When you get to the new place, it will be easy to account for everything.

Don't haul anything empty. Got luggage? Fill it, then move it. Try to fill any empty spaces. Stuff shoes with socks, and boots with shoes. You'll be walking miles with all the trips carrying stuff out of your apartment and into the new one, so anything that reduces the number of trips is a good thing.

LIFTING AND CARRYING

DEFYING GRAVITY

Once it's packed, you'll have to move it. This is where the real fun begins!

LARGE, HEAVY, AND AWKWARD STUFF

You'll learn the answer to two important questions when you have to move something really big and heavy. How much do you really want it? And how many good friends do you have?

Take that old sleeper sofa. (There are few things heavier than a sleeper sofa.) Do you really want it or need it in your new place? (If so, here's a trick—open it up and take the mattress out. It'll be a lot lighter and easier to move.) If you really don't need it, though, you can save yourself a lot of sweat and bloody knuckles deciding that now.

When you're moving big and heavy stuff, use wheels when you can. Piano dollies are carpeted platforms on wheels. Set your dresser on the dolly and wheel it out. Movers' hand trucks look like bigger versions of the hand trucks UPS drivers use, and they have straps that wrap around stuff (like your refrigerator) to secure it. You can rent either from any place that rents moving vans.

Some big stuff disassembles and is much easier to deal with in pieces. Shelves come out of bookcases and entertainment centers. Drawers come out of dressers and desks. My old Steelcase desk weighs a frickin' ton even with the drawers pulled out. Fortunately it breaks apart into four big pieces that I can carry alone; otherwise I'd be out of friends by now.

A few other tricks for big and heavy stuff: Lift it from a low point, if you can. When you're carrying something, you want your arms straight, below your waist, not bent up by your chest. When you lift, keep your back straight. If something's too heavy, stop. Get more help, then move it. When two or more people are carrying something, let the person walking backward set the pace. If you're dealing with stairs, remember that the person on the downhill side takes all of the weight.

GETTING HELP

The better prepared you are to move, the easier it will be to get help. Nobody wants to stand around while you sort and pack.

I always help friends and co-workers move when they ask, because then they'll help me when I need it. So the first trick to getting help moving is to help others. (Besides, it lets you practice loading a truck with their stuff instead of your own.) Bribery also works. If you've got furniture you're not taking or even food that's not making the trip, offer it to the folks helping you. (It's a gratuity, not a bribe.) Keep your workers fed—burgers or a big bucket of chicken goes a long way to keeping people happy and energetic. Serve soda until the truck is loaded, and if you're going to switch to beer, do that at the other end.

Also plan your loading and unloading with your volunteer help in mind. If you can load the front half of your truck with boxes and stuff you can handle yourself, do it. Schedule your help so they arrive when you need them for the really big stuff. Together you load that last and unload it first at the other end, and then you can send your helpers home. Chances are they'll stay until the truck is empty anyway. And more importantly, chances are they'll help you move again in a year or so because you made it so easy for them.

RENTING A TRUCK

GEAR JAMMIN'

Whether or not you'll want to rent a truck comes down to how much stuff you have to move, how far you have to move it, and how much you can afford to spend to move.

If you're not moving much or moving far, you're probably better off making multiple trips in your car. (You can fit an amazing amount of stuff in your car when you really try.) You can also reuse boxes, suitcases, and the like if you unload them between trips. If there are one or two things you can't fit into or tie onto your car—a mattress or bookcase—enlist the aid of someone who owns a truck. (If they own a truck, they expect it.) The fewer the number of heavy items they need to help carry and the more pizza and beer you offer to buy, the more likely they'll be to say yes.

I like to move certain things in my car even if I'm renting a truck. Old-style TVs fit nicely on a car seat (screen facing backward), and the soft seat and suspension protect them. Desktop computers travel nicely this way as well. Food from your refrigerator shouldn't be packed in a truck, which seems obvious but gets overlooked during the chaos of a move. (Pillsbury biscuit rolls explode with a quite frightening BANG! if you let them get too warm.)

If you have too much stuff or are moving too far to make multiple trips feasible, renting a truck may be your only option.

GET A DEAL

There are a lot of places to rent trucks, and not all of them are named U-Haul. Check the local yellow pages under *moving*. Rental car places often have pickups and small vans. Home improvement stores rent trucks and trailers. It's worth shopping around.

Rent the smallest truck that will work. A van or 10-foot truck will get most people out of an apartment, and 12- or 14-footers are available if you have a lot of stuff. The reason you want the smallest truck you can make work is that not only will it be a lot cheaper, you want it full. Remember, tight is safe, loose isn't. You want your truck packed tightly so when you go around a turn or up a hill, nothing shifts or slides.

Some places rent by the day with unlimited miles, some have mileage charges. If you're going a really long way, you may have to pay one-way fees to leave the truck there. (Be sure to plot out all the various mileage charges and plans to find the best deal.) I normally decline the optional insurance when I rent a car, but I get it when I rent a moving van. They're big and awkward and often drive like leaden tanks. The optional insurance is cheap peace of mind.

DRIVING THE RIG

There are a few things to remember when you're driving a moving truck, especially the first couple of times. The first is to use your mirrors.

In a moving truck, there is no rear-view mirror. You have to set the side mirrors on both doors so you can see behind you before you drive away. Not only will you need them to change lanes and back into your driveway to load the truck up, you need them to turn in tight spaces. The truck is going to be longer than your car, and if you're not careful it's easy to scrape it against poles and gates and stoplights if you cut a turn too sharp. The mirrors can help warn you before that optional damage insurance comes into play.

Set the radio to some country station. The older the truck—and the more worn out the suspension—the twangier you'll want the music. (Greasy NASCAR caps and chewing tobacco are entirely up to you.)

When you're driving, give yourself lots of extra room and time to brake. It's partly physics—the more weight you're trying to stop, the longer it takes. It's also the nature of rental trucks. They get abused badly and may not stop as well as they could or should. Also, you want to be as smooth as possible during stops, starts, and turns. The harder and sharper you change directions, the more your stuff will get thrown around inside the truck. Go smooth and easy and use turnout lanes if traffic is backing up behind you.

Before you return a truck, sweep it out, make sure the dollies you rented with it are inside, and refill the tank just before you drop it off. Do not, however, stand outside by the gas pump until the pump shuts off automatically. These trucks have big gas tanks, and they will often show full on the gauge long before they're totally topped off. Put enough gas in the tank to get the gauge back up to where it was when you picked up the truck. Any more is just wasting your money.

ODDS AND ENDS

SMALL STUFF WORTH SWEATING

When you move out, make sure to leave time to clean the place after your stuff is out. Landlords don't just like it, they charge you a fortune if you don't. If you've broken anything or painted a wall or changed a lock or done anything else that is going to cost you your security deposit, now is the time to deal with it. Also, if you're switching over your utilities from one place to another, you might want to consider overlapping for a day or two. It's hard to clean when the water and electricity are both shut off.

It's a good idea to pack an overnight bag with all the stuff you need for a couple of days whenever you move. You do not want to tear apart a loaded truck to find contact lens solution. You will want clean clothes handy because by the end of the day yours are gonna stink. Make sure you've got your checkbook, ATM card, and cash where you can get to them. Cash on hand makes everything go more smoothly.

If there's something big you want to do to your new place—

clean the carpet or paint a room—it's easier before you've filled it with stuff. It's hard to plan for that kind of time, but it is more efficient. (I never can. I try, but it never works out.)

Get signed out of your old place as soon as it's empty and clean. You're not there anymore, and if some jackass breaks in to steal fixtures or just trash the place, you don't want to be held responsible. If you've got a camera phone, take pictures of the clean and empty apartment. If something does happen to it before you and the landlord meet, you've got something at least.

Speaking of safety, keep an eye on your moving truck when it's filled with everything you own. They're easy to steal, anonymous, and ubiquitous. It's not a bad idea to put a padlock on it if you're going to park it for any time at all. Also, make sure you're happy with the locks at your new place before you move your stuff in. Thieves who see you moving in might come in just behind you when you drive that big empty truck away. Because you're moving into a new place, the neighbors won't know you yet and won't know the scruffy guy carrying a box isn't with you.

Beyond that, don't sweat the small stuff. Moving is expensive, heavy, hot, hard work. If most everything makes it to the other side and no one gets hurt, you're ahead of the game. Set your new place up just the way you want it and forget the move ever happened.

CHAPTER 6:

PAINTING

I love paint. It's absolutely the cheapest bang for your buck you'll ever find in making any space—even an apartment—look different, look new, and look clean. (And I think it smells great too, but maybe that's just me.) Walk into a freshly painted room—even a closet—and you'll feel better about being there, you really will.

I know your lease probably says you can't paint. I'm going to show you how you can.

COLOR

FORBIDDEN FRUIT

If you're in a rental, chances are the walls are white, dingy, and pretty unattractive. Maybe you're lucky and the place was just repainted before you moved in. In that case, the walls are just white. In either case, if you want to do something about it, you have some options.

Option 1: Ask permission. Take the paint chip and your plea to you landlord and ask for permission to paint a room, a wall, whatever it is you want to change. The older the paint is already and the less radical the color you propose, the better your chances will be. Offer to buy the paint and do the work. The worst thing that can happen is the landlord says no. If he does say yes, get it in writing so there's no dispute later when you move out.

Option 2: Just do it. This was the option I usually took, but it does have some caveats. First, either limit your color choices to whites or off-whites, or you will have to repaint or pay to have the place repainted when you move out.

Why would you paint white walls white again? Because a fresh, new coat of paint will make the place brighter, cheerier, cleaner, and nicer. If your place is dingy and dull, there's no law (or lease agreement) that says it has to stay that way.

Also, there are literally hundreds of whites and off-whites, so if you find one you really like, go for it. (My personal favorite is a Sherwin Williams color called Bauhaus Buff.) As long as you paint everything with it—so there's no contrast for a landlord to see—no one will ever notice on a move-out walkthrough.

What if you don't want everything white? What if you want a dramatic red accent wall or a baby-blue bedroom? You can still do it—but you have to be prepared to paint the room back to the color it was before you move out. Keep in mind what moving is like—all the hassle and stress and packing and cleaning and loading and moving. It's never fun or easy or fast. If you're convinced you can handle a quick repaint during all of that, then go ahead and paint. (My advice if you do: Leave the trim alone. Trim takes time, and chances are it's white already and white trim will look good with whatever color you're putting up.)

CHOOSING COLORS

Color affects how rooms look and feel. Dark colors make a space feel smaller and more intimate. I painted a small dining room in a rental house brick red once, and it was wonderful at dinner time. (It wasn't great for breakfast, though, because it wasn't as bright and light and cheery as it had been painted white.) Be prepared for those kinds of trade-offs.

One exception to dark colors making a room feel smaller is when you paint just one wall some dark color. That can actually give the illusion of distance and make a space seem larger.

Bright colors have the opposite effect, making rooms seem larger and brighter. But consider the room as well as the color. Get too bright a baby blue in your bedroom, and it's like trying to sleep in an open-cockpit airplane surrounded by BRIGHT BLUE SKY ALL THE TIME. Even birds don't want bright blue sky all the time.

When you choose paint, know that the color will look a lot darker and a lot *more* on your wall than it does on that little chip. A little chip is one square inch or so. A wall is 80 or 120 square feet or so. It's a big difference. If there's a color you really like on a chip, buy the shade one or two steps up from it on the same card. All the colors on a card are the same hue, just different intensities. Picking a lighter hue will give you just the effect you're looking for.

Some paints are also available in little trial sizes. They'll cover a three-by-three-foot section of your wall, which is usually enough to give you a decent concept of what it'll look like when the whole room is that shade. If you worry that the three-by-three section is a little too dark or a little too bright, it is. It'll only be more pronounced when the whole wall is a solid color.

Beyond that, have at it. Color is in these days. My sister's kitchen is a bright cacophony of blues, oranges and yellows, and people say it looks like a Caribbean restaurant. The funny thing is that after she painted it, she started cooking for the first time. She's now taking advanced cooking classes, growing her own vegetables, and even raising chickens in her backyard!

The lesson is to pick colors you like—colors that make you happy—and ignore the worried comments of color-phobic naysayers! (Unless it's your roommate; then work it out.) If afterward you end up with chickens named Buffy, Spike, and Angel pecking around on your back lawn, so much the better!

BUYING WHAT YOU NEED

LET'S GO SHOPPING

It doesn't take a huge investment to do a good paint job, and you don't need that many tools. Here are the ones you have to have.

BRUSHES
Even though you'll be doing most of the work with a roller, you still need a brush for corners and edges. If you're painting trim, you'll need a brush for that as well. If you're not doing trim, you only need one brush: a two-and-a-half- or three-inch synthetic-bristle brush **(see illustration, page 156)**. (It'll say "For Latex Paints.")

You'll use this brush to put paint into the corners where a roller can't go, around light fixtures and switches, and up against the trim (which you'll have neatly taped off). Handles come in many shapes, so pick up a few different brushes and pantomime painting the store wall to find one that fits your hand comfortably. You can spend $3 or $20 for this brush. If you don't plan on doing any more painting anytime soon and don't want to store a paintbrush, buy a cheap one and throw it away when you're done. (It makes cleanup go much faster!) If you think that's environmentally irresponsible, buy a higher quality brush. Take care of it, and it'll last for years.

To paint trim, you need an angled sash brush, one-and-a-half inches wide **(see illustration, page 156)**. The angle of the bristles lets you see the edge you're painting, and the tip of the bristles gets into those hard-to-reach corners. Once again, I recommend you do not paint the trim in a rental, unless the landlord has given you permission. Trim takes forever. In the average interior paint job, painting one coat on the trim takes as long as painting two coats on the walls. If you have to repaint before you move out, you do not want to spend a day-and-a-half tediously painting trim.

There are dozens of different kinds and sizes of brushes, of course, and professional painters carry many, many more. But any pro out there could paint your whole building with just those two, and they're all you really need.

ROLLERS AND PANS

The brush is for getting paint into narrow areas a roller can't reach. The roller is for getting paint everywhere else.

PARTS OF A ROLLER:
• The question-mark-shaped frame or handle.
• The nappy roller cover, which applies the paint.
• The pan, which you need to get paint on the roller.

A lot of places bundle these up and sell them as a set, and that's usually the cheapest way to go. However, as with brushes, different handles will be more or less comfortable for you, and I strongly recommend getting the one that fits you best. (The last thing you want is a blister or for your hand to go numb when you're only half done painting your ceiling . . .) Also, make sure the roller handle has threads formed into the end so you can screw in a broomstick extension. It's easier (and far safer) to paint a ceiling using an extension than climbing up on a ladder.

Roller covers come in various thicknesses. Short-haired, thin ones leave a smoother finish, but don't put up as much paint before they need to be reloaded. They also don't fill cracks and imperfections well.

I prefer thick roller covers. Thick rollers put a lot more paint on your wall before you have to go back to the paint pan and reload them, and they cover rough walls better. They leave an almost dimpled finish on your walls (if you look close), which has never bothered me. Walls are textured anyway, so why shouldn't the paint be a part of it?

Pans are made from aluminum or plastic. I prefer aluminum. Step backward onto an aluminum pan and you'll dent it. Do it on a plastic pan and you'll break it—and a half-gallon of interior latex paint will instantly find the carpet.

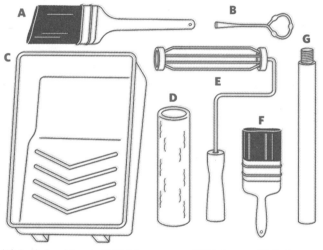

(A) Angled sash brush (B) Paint can opener (C) Roller pan (D) Roller cover
(E) Roller frame (F) Basic brush (G) Broom stick extension

TAPE, DROP CLOTHS, AND OTHER PROTECTION

Remember what your high-school sex-ed teacher said about always using protection? Same thing goes for painting. Use it. You can paint without it, but it only takes that one time for you to really, really regret it.

What protection do you need? Just two things really: painter's tape and drop cloths.

PAINTER'S TAPE

Painter's tape is a special masking tape that's not as sticky. It comes up easier and doesn't pull paint up with it. It's usually blue, but different companies use different colors. Your big decision will be the width of the roll to get. The thin rolls, one-inch wide, are easier to work with. A two-inch-wide roll covers and protects more. I usually have both and end up using the one-inch tape more often.

DROP CLOTHS

If you're using a roller, you need drop cloths. As you roll paint onto the walls and ceiling, tiny droplets fly off the back side of the roller. (They will get in your hair unless you wear a hat.) Without a drop cloth, those little droplets will get on the furniture and carpet and anything else you left uncovered.

There is no law, however, that says you have to buy a drop cloth. Old sheets work just fine. (Unless you really spill on them. Paint will soak through a sheet if you let it.) You can get old flat sheets at any thrift store for sofa change, and donate them back when you're done. (How's that for recycling!) Paint stores sell thin plastic drop cloths that also do the job, but I don't like them on the carpet. They tend to move as you walk on them and pull away from the walls, which defeats the purpose of having them there to begin with. I recommend using sheets on the ground, and the disposable plastic ones to cover furniture.

You can use sheets to cover everything of course, if you have enough old sheets. I'm sure your roommate wouldn't mind . . .

CLEANERS

You need to wash your walls before you paint them because paint doesn't stick well to dirt. Besides, the "I have to stay in and wash my hair" excuse is getting lame. "I have to stay home and wash my walls"—now that's a new and fresh way to turn down a date!

Look for a product called TSP substitute. (The original TSP contained phosphates before we knew they were bad for the planet.) There are no-rinse versions available, if you're philosophically opposed to rinsing recently washed walls.

PAINT

When you buy paint, you have more choices than just the color. There's cheap paint and there's good paint and there's pro paint and there's dull paint and shiny paint and low-odor paint and water-based paint and oil-based paint—and that's just the paint you use on your walls!

LATEX

Let's make it easy. Buy latex paint. It's water-based, which makes cleanup easier. (You don't need paint thinner for water-based paints.) Most of the house paint you'll find in hardware stores is latex, but not quite all. You want latex.

I think cheap paint is among the worst wastes of time ever devised on this earth. Sisyphus could just have easily been condemned to paint with cheap paint instead of having to push a big rock up a hill, and he wouldn't have been any less frustrated. Cheap paint doesn't cover, doesn't dry smooth, and you end up having to use more paint and take more time to do a worse job. It's a bad idea.

Buy decent paint, any national brand. Ace, Sherwin Williams, Behr, True Value. It's all $15 to $20 a gallon, and all works well. (This is one of those times when being a good shopper can really pay off. Paint goes on sale, and when it does you can save $5 a gallon or so. Sales are common in the spring and before almost all three-day weekends.)

SHEEN

Sheen is another choice, and it determines how shiny the paint is when you're done. Sheens start at flat, which is a dull finish, and go through a progression of eggshell, satin, semi-gloss, and gloss. The shinier the paint, the tougher the finish, and the easier it will be to clean. Shinier paint is also more expensive than flatter finishes because shiny paints contain more solids and are more expensive to make. Chances are your apartment is painted with a flat paint. Eggshell will look nicer and clean up easier. (So will satin, but your landlord will notice that difference.) Bathrooms and kitchens should be semi-gloss, and trim is usually gloss.

CALCULATE

The last decision you'll have to make is how much paint to buy. Two gallons will usually do a small bedroom. (Usually, but there are so many variables you can never be 100 percent sure ahead of time.) There are online paint calculators out there, but the best way to know is to buy your paint from a paint store or a small neighborhood hardware store where the guys and gals at the paint counter actually know something about paint. Tell them what you're painting and give them a decent idea of the size of your rooms, and they'll steer you in the right direction.

If you're buying a standard in-stock color, you can return unopened cans; buying an extra gallon to be safe won't hurt. (Custom-mixed colors are not usually returnable.) Nice paint-counter people usually throw in a couple of free stir sticks and a paint-can opener. If they don't, ask!

No matter how much you buy, it's almost impossible to buy just enough. Either you'll find yourself running out—and squeezing every last drop out of the can and roller tray hoping it'll cover—or you'll have three-quarters of a gallon left over. It happens to everyone.

PREPARATION

GET READY, GET SET

By now you're probably beginning to get the idea that painting is a pain in the posterior. You're not wrong. It is. But it's still the easiest and cheapest home/apartment makeover you can do. There is some prep work you're going to need to do before opening the paint cans, and it'll make the painting easier and the outcome better.

For planning purposes, figure one afternoon to one day for prep, and one full day to paint a room or two.

FURNITURE

Two options here—get it out of the room entirely, or push it all to the center of the room (stacking is okay) and work around it. Do whatever works best for your particular situation. If you leave furniture in the room, make sure to cover it.

WALLS

There are several things you need to do to ready your walls, and the first is to take everything off them. Pictures, posters, sombreros—whatever you've got up there. Pull the nails and screws out too (they can tear up a roller), and if you think you might put stuff back in a different place, fill the holes with spackle. (This is covered in the Apartments chapter, page 125.) If you do spackle, you really should let it dry before you paint it. Overnight is fine.

You also need to take off the switch plate covers and electrical outlet covers and phone jack covers and any other kind of plastic cover screwed into your wall. They are held on with one or two slotted screws. (Use a hand screwdriver to put them back on when you're done. With a power driver, it's easy to tighten them too much and break the switch plate.) You can keep the plates and their screws separate—sandwich bags are great for this—or throw them all together in a shoebox and sort it out afterward. If they're filthy, soaking them in a little ammonia and water solution works wonders.

WASHING

Now you gotta wash the walls. Get out your TSP substitute and follow the directions and have at it. I usually put drop cloths down before washing to keep the water off the carpet or floor. You don't have to scrub every mark off the wall, just make sure the solution gets wiped everywhere. Use a mop if you've got one. I know this section is about walls, but you should wash your ceiling, too, especially in a kitchen or bathroom. (Ever take a close look right above a stove or shower? Paint doesn't stick to those little grease droplets.) Obviously you don't need to wash it if you're not painting it, or if it's that real bumpy popcorn texture stuff.

In addition to removing dirt, TSP substitutes takes the sheen off the old coat of paint, which helps the new paint stick better.

MASKING

Masking is the slowest part of prep work, but it speeds up the painting considerably, so it's well worth it.

WHAT TO MASK?

Masking a doorway

Start with the trim. Even if you're going to paint the trim (don't do it!) you'll want to mask it off. If you don't, the wall paint will get on the trim and form a ridge that'll be visible after you paint the trim. It's better to mask it off.

Trim includes the frames around doors and windows, baseboards, etc. If you're painting the baseboards with wall paint, mask off the carpet and·tape down your drop cloths. Mask off light fixtures (and take the glass covers down.) Basically look around the room and put tape or newspaper (or tape and newspaper) anywhere you don't want paint.

PAINT!

COLOR YOUR WORLD

Finally, after all that prep, it's time to paint. Set your paint can on something flat and stable, and put a whole opened newspaper under it. Use the little opener the nice paint counter person gave you to pry off the lid. (A screwdriver works, too.) Take a stir stick and give your paint a nice stir. Use your brush to wipe the paint off the stir stick, and set the stick on top of the paint can lid.

Now take off your shoes.

I'm actually not kidding. If you drip or spill paint on the drop cloth—especially a plastic one—and then step in it with your shoes, you won't notice it, and you risk tracking paint all around. I've seen it happen. If you're painting barefoot or in socks, you'll feel the paint on your feet before you trod down the hall.

PAINTING ORDER

1 . The first thing you're going to do is use your three-inch brush to paint all the corners and edges where a roller can't reach or a roller can cause problems. Basically, you're outlining your walls and ceiling with a three-inch border of paint (it's called cutting in). Just above the baseboards. Around the edges of your doors and windows. Around each and every electrical outlet and light fixture. In the corners where the walls meet, and the overhead corner where the ceiling meets the walls.

When you paint with a brush, dip it about a third of the way into the paint, then wipe the edges of the brush on the inside lip of the can. Too much paint on your brush will drip off and make a mess.

2 . Once you've got the outlining done, you're going to begin rolling. Make sure the roller pan is also somewhere flat and stable, and put a full newspaper under it as well. Put the roller cover on the roller handle, and pour paint into the pan until the deep end is full. Dip the roller into the paint.

You want the whole roller full of paint, so you have to roll it into the edge of the paint in your pan. When you first dip it, one side gets heavy and the roller may not roll. Use your fingers to turn the roller to get the dry side in the paint, then it should be fine.

 **3** . When you paint a whole room, start with the ceiling. Pick a corner and take your roller and make a two to three-foot "M" in that corner **(see illustration)**. (You can make a "W" if you feel like it.) Now roll back over it to fill in the empty spaces, and you should have a solid two-to-three-foot square in the corner.

Now make another next to it, and another, and another. Painting is like eating a dinosaur—you do it one bite at a time.

When you've worked your way all the way along the wall, go back to your starting point and make the next row of three-foot Ms in the same direction as your first. Whenever possible, you want to keep a "wet-edge" and work your way down a ceiling or wall adding coverage to paint that's still wet.

Don't be surprised if it takes nearly half of your paint to cover the ceiling. It's a big expanse and isn't broken up by doors and windows. And don't get discouraged if it takes a while. It's the biggest part of the job. Once you've got the ceiling painted, you're more than halfway done.

Another thing—don't freak out if the color you see isn't the color on the chip. As paint dries, it changes. You won't know for sure what it's going to look like until it's all dry.

4 . Once the ceiling is painted, pick a wall, start in a top corner, and make more Ms. (Or Ws if you're that kind of person.) Fill the walls in the same square-by-square pattern, working down from the top of the wall. If you've masked corners and obstructions off well and cut in all your edges, it'll go fast. If there are a few areas still hard to reach with a roller, use your brush.

If you get a drip where you don't want it, wipe it up with a damp washcloth. As long as it's still wet, you can make it disappear completely.

5 . Will you need a second coat? A lot of paints promise one-coat coverage, and some actually deliver. You will have to wait until your first coat is dry before you'll be able to tell if you need a second coat. If the paint looks blotchy and uneven, or if you see little bits of the original color peeking through, you need a second coat.

The good thing about second coats is they go on much faster than first coats, and use far less paint. And they always make a room look better. I plan on doing a second coat whenever I paint. If you do paint a second coat, you'll be glad you did.

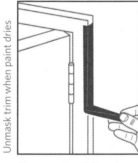

Unmask trim when paint dries

6 . If you're going to paint trim, paint it last. Unmask it, mask off the walls (once they're good and dry), pick a corner, and work your way around the room. It's slow work, and you can't speed it up without making a mess, so just be slow and steady and neat.

Guess what? You just painted a room.

CLEAN UP

GET CLEAN AFTERWARD

The final step in painting is the clean up. If you've got a bucket or something like one, fill it with water and soak your brush and roller while you do everything else first. It'll make them easier to clean later.

Carefully pull up all the masking tape and turn back the drop cloths and roll or fold them up. Put the switch plates back up, the furniture back in place, and the light shades on.

PAINT ON CARPET

If you drip paint on your carpet and see it while it's still wet, use your fingers and a damp cloth and try to get below it and squeeze it up out of the carpet. (The last thing you want to do is spread it around.) If you don't notice it until it's dry, get out a pair of scissors and clip it out. No one notices a tiny divot or a missing carpet fiber. Everyone notices a white speck. If you have a really low, flat carpet, you can (carefully) scrape a knife over it to flake the dried paint off.

CLEANING BRUSHES

Cleaning brushes just takes time and water. I use a hose outside where the water will soak into a lawn or dirt bed and not wash off into the storm drain. Run water over the bristles of your brush until it comes off clear. It takes a good long while, but if you don't get it clean now, it'll be a stiff mess next time you go to use it. Rollers take even longer, but a good soak first really helps. Wash out the roller pan as well. (There might be some dried paint stuck to the top edge that doesn't come off, but that won't hurt anything.)

If you bought really cheap brushes and don't plan on using them again, leave the brush and roller cover in the roller pan until they're dry, then throw them away.

That's all there is to it! Save any leftover paint for touch-ups down the road, and be proud of a job well done.

CHAPTER 7:

DECORATING

Since you've gone to all the trouble of painting your apartment, you may as well make the rest of it look nice, too. The good thing is that it's not that hard or that expensive to do some basic decorating—including resurrecting flea market furniture.

TRASH TO TREASURE

FLEA MARKET FABU

While it's true people toss out a lot of junk, they also get rid of some surprisingly good stuff as well. The trick is knowing where—and when—to look.

FINDING THE GOOD STUFF
FLEA MARKETS

Most towns have one or have one nearby. They're usually on the weekend (but not always) and usually free or a buck or two to get in. Bring cash, and always take a friend to a flea market. Not only will they be able to help you carry stuff, they'll save you money.

You can get decent stuff at flea markets, but you can over-pay, too. Some vendors think "old" means "antique" and try to charge accordingly. Don't let them. A good strategy is to walk the whole grounds first before dealing on anything. If you're looking for a dresser, get a sense of what dressers are selling for. There will be a range.

Here's where the friend comes in. Now that you know what dressers are going for, go to the vendor who has the one you want. If it's the cheapest, pay the man and get your friend to carry one end. If it's not, ask the seller how much he's charging, then ask your friend what he or she thinks.

The conversation should go something like this:

You: "$30 seems okay. What do you think?"

Your Friend: "For that? Didn't you see the one by the food carts? Way prettier (or better/bigger/in better shape) and it was only $20."

You: "Really? Show me."

The Vendor: "I'll take $20 for this one if you buy it right now."

You: "$20 for the dresser and that poster (or dish rack/clock radio/whatever else it is you need) and you've got a deal."

It works. Sellers at flea markets and garage sales have to load up anything they don't sell, and all of them face the very real possibility that some of their junk will never sell.

So they're loath to turn down a cash offer. And while they'll only bend so far on a price, they'll almost always toss in an extra thing if you ask. And if not, so what? If the dresser's a good deal at $20, buy it. If not, keep looking.

GARAGE SALES

Garage sales work a lot like flea markets (and the same wheeling-dealing rules apply) but they're spread out and somewhat inefficient. But if you're up early some spring Saturday morning and really need dishes, you can do worse then cruising the 'burbs looking at garage sale stuff.

CRAIGSLIST.COM

Craig's List is great because it takes about two seconds to check, you can often see photos, and you may find better quality castoffs than you'll get at garage sales. Sometimes the prices are great, sometimes not. At least you know the thing you're looking for is actually for sale and don't waste a lot of time and gas driving around hoping someone will have the perfect desk, dresser, or nightstand at their garage sale.

THRIFT STORES

Thrift stores are a very good option. Not only do they sell furniture, small appliances, and other household goods, they keep regular hours, update their stock fairly frequently, and even have sales. I got a Steelcase desk at a thrift store about 20 years ago for $12.50 (and still use the beast today).

MOVE-OUT WEEKEND

This is always my favorite. Go to any college town the weekend after finals and take a pickup. Desks, chairs, dressers—you name it, it'll be out on the edge of the street. Most of it is crap, of course, but not all. And if it's your town and you're not moving out, so much the better. You can literally walk perfectly good furniture home for free.

RECOGNIZING THE GOOD STUFF

When you're examining furniture, there are a few things to consider. First, obviously, is does it work or can you make it work? If it's a bed frame, does it hold together? Do the drawers in a desk or dresser open and close? Are all the pieces there, and if not, are the missing ones pieces you can live without?

CONDITION AND CONSTRUCTION

Second is condition and construction. There are two basic kinds of furniture construction—solid wood and pressed wood. Solid wood is just that—furniture made of boards and planks of solid wood, or of plywood (which is thin layers of wood glued together). With plywood, the outside layer can be high-quality wood and stained or varnished so the grain of the wood shows.

Pressed wood is made of small fibers of wood—waste generated at mills and shops—that is pressed together with

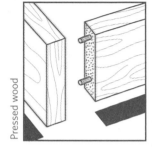

Pressed wood

glue and pressure. Pressed wood isn't pretty, so it won't be stained or varnished. It can be painted, but will often be covered with a durable paper that's been printed to look like wood. It's a cheaper way to make furniture, and most of the shelves, desks, and book-cases you can buy at Wal Mart, Ikea, Target, or Staples are built this way.

KNOWING HOW IT'S MADE

Knowing how a piece of furniture is made is important for a couple of reasons. The first is for repair purposes. Some-times pressed wood boards split, usually along a joint where screws or other connectors held one piece to another piece. These breaks are very hard to repair. Also, if the cov-ering paper is damaged or peeling, there's really not a whole lot you can do. Think about where you'd put the desk or bookcase or whatever it is, and if the ugly part will show. If not, drag it home. If it will, you'll have to weigh how much you value functional and free against ugly and tacky.

Solid wood furniture gives you greater options. It'll either be stained—you can see the wood grain—or painted. If it's stained but ugly, you can paint it or even stain it a darker color if you are willing to do a little more work. If it's already painted, repainting is your only realistic option. (You can strip the paint, sand, and stain, but it's a lot of work and you need a safe place to do it.)

WHAT TO LOOK FOR

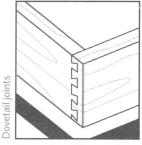
Dovetail joints

So what do you look for in a piece of furniture? How solid it feels. How tight the drawers are—are they solid boxes, or do they feel like they're about to fall apart? (Dovetail joints on the front edge of a drawer—they'll look like incomplete triangles—are an indication of quality and craftsmanship.)

Are the legs of a chair all tight and solid? Is there obvious damage, and if so, how well will you be able to fix it, replace it, or hide it?

And I always look for ugly.

Yep, ugly is your friend. Let's say you're a guy, and you have a guy's apartment, and you need a dresser. Your best deal will come on the baby-blue and pink dresser stenciled with angels and roses—something so frou-frou even your grandmother would gag. Why? Because under the hideous paint may well be a perfect dresser—strong and solid and well-built. Add a coat of paint, and you'll have a $300 dresser for $30.

REPAINTING

If you've found a piece you like and want to freshen it up, a new coat of paint can work wonders. It's also not too hard.

PREPARATION

No matter what the piece of furniture is, the preparation steps are pretty much the same. Take any knobs or pulls off, unless they are going to be painted the same color as the rest. (If that's the case, just leave them on and paint them in place.) Take out any drawers and set them aside to paint the fronts separately.

The rest of the steps are best done in a garage or on a patio, but if the only place you have to work is your kitchen or living room floor, so be it. You will need to put down lots of newspaper or old sheets, and vacuum more than once to keep the dust down.

1 . Before you paint, you have to make sure the paint will stick to the old finish. And that means cleaning it up and dulling it down. To clean it, just scrub it down with dish soap and a dish scrubby. You can use stronger degreasers like Simple Green or one of the citrus degreasers if the dresser or desk or whatever it is really grungy, but you probably won't need to.

2 . Once the piece is clean, it's a good idea to sand it lightly with 180- or 220-grit sandpaper. (This is also called "fine" sandpaper.) This is especially important if you're painting over a stained finish. After staining, furniture is usually top-coated with some kind of hard, clear finish—varnish, lacquer, or the like. Paint doesn't stick well to any very smooth surface. Sanding lightly with fine sandpaper will create millions of small grooves in the old finish that will let the paint stick. Sand in one direction, with the grain of the wood or with the brush strokes if the piece is painted.

3 . When you've sanded it all, wipe it down with a very lightly damp cloth to get up all the dust. It's best if your cloth is damped with mineral spirits instead of water, but water works if you don't have mineral spirits. (The problem with water on bare wood—if the old finish is entirely gone—is that it will raise the grain of the wood, and it'll feel rough again.) So keep your rag barely damp—just enough to trap dust. If water does raise the grain, sand the rough spots over again, then just wipe away the dust with a dry cloth.

PAINTING

1 . Once the piece is clean and sanded, paint it with any quality interior paint your heart desires. A quart will usually be plenty. Watch the edges for drips, and smooth them out with your brush before they dry. If you want to paint it in some wild multi-color scheme, look for the small trial-size jars of paint rather than having custom colors mixed at a higher cost.

2 . Two coats are better than one; just let the paint dry between coats. When you're painting multiple coats, you don't have to clean your paintbrush between coats. Just wrap it well in aluminum foil, sealing the bottom and top edges. The foil keeps the wet paint on the brush wet for a full day or so, letting you get to the second coat in a reasonable amount of time. If you need more time, you're better off cleaning the brush.

3 . Once the paint is dry, reinstall any knobs or pulls you removed—all you'll need is a screwdriver—put the drawers back in place, and set the piece wherever you want it to live. One thing to be careful of: The paint inside any paint drips that may have formed may still be wet even though the rest of the piece is dry. If a drip formed on the bottom edge of the piece and you didn't notice, moving it too soon can cause the drip to open like a scab and let wet paint stain your carpet.

4 . One more caution: Even though your paint will be dry to the touch, it won't be fully cured and hardened for two or three days. Let it sit that long before you start stacking a bunch of stuff on it, or you'll risk having your stuff stick to your newly painted desk!

RECOVERING SEATS

One of the easiest flea-market fixes to do is recovering tacky chairs or barstool seats. Recovering an overstuffed sofa or La-Z-Boy recliner is not easy—we're talking about desk and dining-room-style chairs here. Here's how.

1 . Flip the chair upside down and see how the seat attaches to the chair. It's usually four screws, each holding one corner in place. Take those out and the seat lifts right off.

2 . You have two choices here: Remove the old upholstery and start over, or just install new fabric (or even new foam and fabric) right over the top of the stuff that's already there. If the existing fabric isn't ripped, textured in some way that will show through, or grimy and funky-smelling, there is no reason not to just put the new fabric over the old.

If you're going to remove the old upholstery, pry up the staples holding it down and throw it and all the staples away. If the old foam or batting (the cottony stuffing stuff) is nasty, throw that away, too.

3 . If you need to replace foam, you can buy it at any fabric department. It comes in different thicknesses, and you can stack layers to get whatever thickness you need. Trim foam with scissors to the exact size and shape of your seat pad.

4 . For fabric, look for something with some heft to it. You don't need official "upholstery" fabric, but you don't want to cover a chair you're actually going to sit on in some delicate lacy fabric, either. If the fabric is plain, lay the fabric face down and place the upside-down seat on top of it. Get a tape measure or ruler and find the exact center of the front edge of the seat, and the exact center of the rear edge. Make a nice pencil mark at both spots. Trim the fabric following the shape of the seat, but leave plenty to wrap around any foam or other padding, and leave an extra inch or even two to fold over and staple on the back.

If you are recovering a seat with a patterned fabric, you'll use your centerlines to line up the pattern and make sure it's straight and centered on each seat you recover. On your fabric, pick the line or print of the pattern you want in the middle of your seat. Place the fabric face down, and set the seat on top of it, also face down. Center the fabric on your seat by folding it over the front edge of the seat and lining up your centerline or pattern on the fabric with the pencil mark you made on the seat base. Check both the front and back, and when they're lined up straight, you're ready to staple.

STAPLE IT DOWN

1. You need a real staple gun for this bit. They sell them at any supercenter or hardware store, and the newer, better ones are more ergonomic and easier to use. (There are even electric ones that are extremely easy to use, but more than you need to do just a few chairs.) When you buy a staple gun, make sure it comes with staples. If your staple gun doesn't have the staple size stamped or formed somewhere on the tool itself, write it on with a Sharpie. Staples come in different sizes, and you will lose the little piece of paper that tells you what size staples to buy by the time you actually need to reload the staple gun again in two years. Having it written on the tool itself is a great timesaver.

2. Okay, now let's upholster. The first staple you drive is the one at the front center, right at your pencil mark. Wrap the fabric over the front edge of the seat, then fold it under itself so it doubles. (It's stronger this way and looks neater.) Hold it down flat, then snap your first staple in. The staples run the same direction as the chair edge.

3. Now go to the back edge. Pull the fabric taut—not super tight, but enough to take out any looseness in the fabric and compress any foam you may have used just a little. Fold over the back edge just like you did the front, and drive a staple into the center back, making sure your pattern lines up to that center mark as well.

4 . Go back to the front edge, and pulling gently to keep the fabric taut, add staples to either side of your center staple. Do the same in the back, and work your way across both the front and back edges.

5 . The sides are a little different. You start the sides in the front corners, folding the fabric over to make a nice, creased corner, then staple it in place. Do each corner, and smooth and pull the fabric gently and work down each side. It's not unlike wrapping a Christmas present. (It is true that I may wrap a little differently than most . . . .) When you get to the final corner, fold the fabric and make that corner as neat and tight as you can. If you mess up or don't like the way the corners look or if the seat is too tight or too loose, all you have to do to start over is pry up your staples and go back to the beginning.

The whole process takes less than an hour, and if you're doing multiple chairs you'll be getting the last few done in ten or twenty minutes each.

SWITCH COVERS AND DRAWER PULLS

SWITCH IT OUT

If your apartment or rental is a hovel, making all your switch plates or drawer pulls match isn't going to do much. (I once looked at a rental that was advertised as a "small country cabin in a rural setting." The correct description would have been "shack." Switch plates wouldn't have helped even if the place had been equipped with electricity . . . .) But if your apartment or rental is nice, new switch plates and outlet covers, and matching drawer and cabinet pulls, will give your place a very nicely finished look and feel.

SWITCH PLATES AND OUTLET COVERS

Switch plates and outlet covers come in a few different colors (tan and white are the most popular) and don't cost much at all. If yours are mismatched, your room will always look unfinished no matter how nicely you've painted it. New covers come with screws, too, so those match as well. As mentioned once before, use a hand screwdriver when installing switch plate and light switch covers. (Power screwdrivers can go too fast and crack them.) If you're really after a professional look, make sure the slots in the screws all point straight up and down. Also, if your covers are okay but missing a screw here or there, you can buy the correct-color screws separately for just a few pennies.

When you're shopping, make a good count and take a list in with you to the hardware store so you don't forget any and have to make a separate trip. Because switch plates come in so many different configurations, I make a quick sketch of what I need rather than trying to describe it, just so there's no confusion once I get to the store.

CABINET HARDWARE
Cabinet hardware is more expensive, but if your knobs and pulls are hideous or broken or missing, they are also an easy-to-install upgrade. (This is one I'd try to get the landlord to pay for or at least split.)

The trick with buying new cabinet hardware is 1) getting the right sized replacements, and 2) making sure the store you're shopping at has or can order everything you need. There's nothing more frustrating than spending a bunch of money and still having mismatched drawer pulls because the store had six and you needed eight.

To make sure you get the right size, take one of each type of pull or handle you're replacing with you. They will have threaded posts sticking out the back, and you want to make sure the new ones have posts in the same place and the same length. To make getting the right number easy, put a piece of masking tape on each of the old pulls and write the number you need on the tape.

REMOVAL AND INSTALLATION

Removal and installation is straightforward. The threaded posts slide through holes drilled in the drawers or cabinet doors, and are held in place by screw-on caps. To remove old hardware, unscrew the caps with whatever type of screwdriver they require. (Either Philips or a flat-head.) If a knob spins as you try to unscrew the cap, hold it with one hand and use your screwdriver with the other.

Installing the new handles and pulls is just as easy. Slide the posts through the holes and spin the caps down over them. Tighten them down pretty good with your screwdriver so the pressure of the cap against the drawer holds everything tight. If a pull starts to feel loose over time, just get out your screwdriver and snug it up.

Et voilà! Your kitchen looks brand spankin' new!

BLINDS AND CURTAINS

SEE THE LIGHT (OR NOT)

Usually blinds and curtains come with a rental, but not always. If yours doesn't have them—or has ones so hideous they just have to go—this section will help you buy and hang new ones.

BLINDS AND SHADES

There are many different kinds of blinds, and the kind that's right for you will be a matter of taste, use, and budget.

BAMBOO SHADES

The cheapest are probably those roll-up bamboo shades, which are also dead-easy to install, but they also look like cheap roll-up bamboo shades. If you've got an island theme going, or are really broke, they work great. These days there are even high-end roll-up bamboo shades that cost more and look a lot more finished.

ROLLER SHADES

A variant on the same theme are roller shades, those old-school shades that pull down and (hopefully) stay, then roll up out of the way. Mini-blinds put a severe crimp in the roller shade market, but these are still a good option. They're not expensive, they're easy to install, and you can pick between ones that let light filter in or ones that really block light and keep your room nice and dark. The only real downside to roller shades is that the roller itself isn't what anyone would call pretty, so people usually use them where they can be hidden behind a curtain valance—that horizontal strip of curtain that runs across the top of the windows.

MINI BLINDS

Mini-blinds have advantages over roller-type shades and blinds. Because they're adjustable, they can let varying amounts of light in, or let light in while still providing privacy. Price-wise, they're more expensive than simpler shades, but not outrageous. And unlike roller shades, they don't look unattractive when they're pulled up.

MEASURING FOR BLINDS

The key decision you have to make when you're buying shades or blinds is if you will install them inside the window frame or outside. Inside the frame is the standard method in newer buildings because it gives a cleaner, built-in look. Outside the frame is required with older casement

Measure for inside-mounted blinds

windows where both the upper and lower halves of the window move. These windows typically have wooden trim around them and are found in older homes and buildings.

INSIDE-MOUNTED BLINDS

1. If you have newer windows set inside what essentially looks like a box built into your wall, you can do inside-mounted blinds. There are two measurements you need to take. The first is side to side: the exact distance between the side walls of your window frame **(see illustration)**. The blinds or shades you buy have to fit neatly inside the frame—not touching the sides, but not leaving so much clearance that light and prying eyes can peek through. The other measurement you need to take is height: the distance from the top of the window frame to the bottom. Absolute accuracy is less critical, but you don't want your shade to be three inches shorter than your window!

2. When you measure width, measure straight across at the top, middle, and bottom of the window frame. (Diagonals are longer than straight lines and will throw things off.) The reason you measure three times is that things aren't always straight and square like they should be. Read the tape measure closely—at least down to the eighth of an inch. Write down the smallest of the three measurements. You're going to want to buy blinds one-half inch less than your window frame width, so accuracy matters.

OUTSIDE-MOUNTED BLINDS

1. For outside-mount blinds, measure the distance outside the window you want the blinds to cover. Outside-mounted blinds are far less critical when it comes to width.

If you have standard-sized windows, you'll be able to find off-the-rack blinds that fit them. You can find them at big hardware stores like Home Depot and Lowes, at paint and decorating stores (where you may pay more), at home stores like Bed Bath and Beyond, and at discount stores like Wal Mart and Target. I'd recommend starting there and seeing if those stores have the size blinds you need. If not, it's a decent bet your windows are not a standard size.

In the past, that used to mean ordering custom blinds, which no one wants to do in a rental. These days, it just means getting standard blinds trimmed, and it's easier than it sounds. At the big box hardware stores, they can trim blinds on the spot. (Well, if you can find anyone to help you, they can . . .) It's handy. If you like those fabric honeycomb-style blinds, you can even buy a kit that comes with a small hand-trimming saw so you can trim them yourself at home.

INSTALLING BLINDS

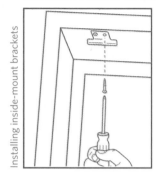

Installing inside-mount brackets

1. When you buy blinds, they will come with mounting brackets. The brackets for inside-mount blinds install inside the window frame, and outside-mount blinds come with brackets that install outside the window frame. (I bet you already guessed that.)

2. The most important piece of the brackets is the instructions. Different blinds have different brackets, and they may install differently. So to get yours right, read, and follow the instructions. Those instructions will tell you how to position them, get them level, and properly secure them to your wall. Sometimes you have to drill small pilot holes for the screws.

Take your time when you're installing brackets for blinds so yours will hang nice and straight.

CURTAINS

Curtains are easy. While it's possible to spend a fortune on curtains, doing so is really rather silly. A curtain is just a piece of cloth hung from a pole or stick across a window. I guess in a designer house going to be featured in *Better*

Homes and Gardens, you'd need to have fancy curtains. In a rented apartment or house, you can do better.

1 . First, decide which windows really need curtains. We had a rental once that had custom curtains in the dining room. Why you'd need heavy curtains in that dining room was never clear to me, so I took them down. There may be windows like that in your place—ones no one can see in without already being in your back or side yard, or ones where you don't care if people can see in anyway.

2 . For the windows where you do want to keep prying eyes (and sunlight) out, you have options. The home stores and discount retailers sell decent curtains at decent prices. And for a rental, you don't need the fancy pull-a-cord-and-they-open kind. Tab-topped curtains that you pull sideways to open work just as well.

RODS

If you're shopping for curtains, the first thing to do is measure your windows, side to side and top to bottom. Unlike inside-mount blinds, the measurements don't require precision down to the fraction of an inch. In fact, you want your curtain rod to extend out past the window by two to three inches on either side. The extra length lets the curtains open fully, and blocks light better when they're closed.

Most curtain rods you can buy are adjustable and come with the brackets you'll need to install them. It's best to screw the brackets into a wooden stud when possible because that's a lot stronger then being screwed·into drywall. The good thing is that builders have to use extra framing around doors and windows, so there's lot of wood just above and beyond the edges of a window to use. (Use a stud sensor to make sure you'll hit wood. If you won't, use a drywall anchor to attach the bracket. See page 124 for more on hardware.)

We went to help my son move into a new apartment once, and one of his roommates was attempting to install curtain rod brackets—with the rod and curtains attached! It wasn't going well. Instead, install the brackets first, with nothing attached to them, then lift the rod and curtains into place.

The one thing you want to try to do when installing curtain brackets is get them all lined up straight. You can use a tape measure and level to do this, or you can cheat and use a common household item as a reference to get the brackets in the same position relative to the window. Your iPod, for instance. The brackets can be aligned one iPod's width above the top of the window frame, and one iPod's length to the left and right. (You can use your TV remote, a box of penne pasta, or a fifth of gin—whatever's handy.) Just make pencil marks on the wall, and align the brackets to those marks. They'll come with screws to install them, or you can use drywall screws if you have some about.

Once the brackets are up, install the curtains on the rod and lift the curtain and rod together into place.

CURTAINS ON THE CHEAP
It used to be that things were cheaper to make than to buy, but that's not always the case any more. Buying yards and yards of raw fabric to make into curtains will probably be a lot more expensive than buying pre-made curtains at a discount retailer or home store. (And then there's the whole sewing thing.) But there are other options, if you're clever.

OPTION 1
Thrift stores are one option. Curtains do end up at thrift stores. And when you think about the life of a curtain—it really just hangs there—there's not a whole lot of wear and tear going on. Creative and artistic types have been known to use thrift store coats as curtains. Thread the rod through the sleeves and you've got something that blocks light and makes a personal statement. Our daughter used a sari for her bedroom curtain for years. People also use ponchos and heavy wool blankets as great curtains.

OPTION 2

For something that looks more curtain-ish, consider bed-spreads or tablecloths. Bedspread curtains have the advantage of matching your bedding perfectly, and table-cloth curtains can be updated seasonally if you want. In both cases, just drape the cloth over the rod, keeping the ends even or at least close to even so one side isn't drastically heavier than the other. To make it look more like a curtain and not a bedspread draped over a curtain rod, you can pin the two sides together with safety pins, or even use iron-on hemming tape. Sandwich the tape between the two sides and follow the directions to fuse them together. Just make sure to leave yourself a pocket for the curtain rod!

One last word about curtains—make sure they actually work. Some fabrics look reasonably thick, but when you put light behind them you can pretty much see right through them. When you've hung new curtains, go outside at night and look through while your roommate or someone moves around the window inside. You do not want the little old lady down the block to be one who lets you know your new curtains are see-through!

CHAPTER 8:

YARD WORK

The great thing about most rentals is that you don't have to do yard work. It's certainly the case in apartment complexes, and most duplexes include basic yard care in the price of your monthly rent.

There are exceptions, though. Some duplexes don't include yard care, and many single-family homes don't as well. Some landlords who do provide yard care will reduce the rent if you offer to maintain the yard yourself. And some people, believe it or not, discover they actually like mowing the lawn. (There are people who get actual college degrees in lawn science and then take care of golf courses and the like.) But you don't need a degree, or even any experience. Keeping a basic lawn looking decent is pretty easy. You've got to cut it, you've got to water it, and once in a while it doesn't hurt to feed it and get the weeds out.

MOWING

JUST A LITTLE OFF THE TOP

If you do have to do yard work at your place, this is probably the work you'll be doing. Fortunately, in most rentals at least, you probably won't have a five-acre estate to take care of.

The idea when you mow is to trim the top third of the grass and keep your lawn about three-and-a-half inches tall—about the width of a credit card. And there are a variety of ways to do it.

MOWERS

You have three choices when it comes to traditional mowers—push mowers, electric mowers, and gas mowers. Each has advantages and disadvantages in terms of ease of use, environmental impact, and cost. We'll look at each, starting with cheap and good for the Earth.

PUSH MOWERS

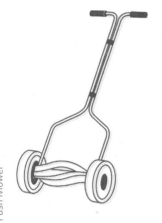

Push Mower

Push mowers are just that—grass cutters that work when you push them. They have kind of an open tube of blades called a reel that spins when the wheels of the mower spin. (The industry, naturally, calls them "reel mowers," under-playing the whole having-to-push-them aspect.) They usually have a small grass catcher that attaches to the back and simple wooden handles and are cheap and absolutely non-polluting. Even better, you can find them in thrift stores for $10 to $20 if you look. (If you do get one second-hand, you might want to take it to a saw shop and have the blades sharpened. It'll cost $30 or so and be well worth it.)

The downside to push mowers is that they are a bit more work to use. You are the motor that makes the blades spin. It's not a workout like going to the gym, but it's not as easy as the stroll behind a self-propelled gas mower, either. Because the grass catcher is small, you do end up having to dump the clippings more often, too. That said, I love push mowers. If your yard is reasonably small and reasonably level, they are the cheapest and most environmentally friendly option by far. And besides, you probably go to a gym or do something to workout anyway. Why not let your Saturday morning workout be a bit of Earth-friendly lawn care instead of a drive to 24-Hour Fitness?

ELECTRIC MOWERS

Electric Mower

Electric mowers are the next-best kind of mower when it comes to price and impact on the environment. Like push mowers, they are also quiet and won't disturb your neighbors. They look like any other modern mower except they have a cord trailing behind.

With both electric and gas mowers, you can find models that mulch the grass clippings and models that bag the clippings. Mulching is better. Mulching mowers whack and cut the grass clipping several times until they're just tiny little nubkins, and then they leave those nubkins on the lawn. The small grass bits fall down between the blades of grass and fertilize the lawn nicely. They also keep green waste out of landfills or county collection stations, and they have the added benefit of letting you skip the whole annoying emptying-the-bag step.

Electric mowers don't have the air pollution problems gas mowers do, but they do have an environmental impact. While it's true that electric mowers (and cars for that matter) run clean, that electricity did have to be generated somehow. If you live somewhere where most of the power is generated by hydroelectric dams, it really is pretty clean (forgetting for a moment whatever might have been permanently flooded when they built the dam in the first place). But if you live somewhere where there are still coal-fired power plants, know that your clean electric mower isn't quite as clean as you might hope.

The other downside to electric mowers is that you are literally tied to an electrical outlet. You can mow only as far as your extension cord will reach. (And you have to keep moving the cord to keep from running over it.) There are rechargeable battery-powered models that free you from the cord, but they are not cheap and tie you to the state of charge in the battery. (Battery production is also not the most environmentally friendly industry in the world, either.)

GAS MOWERS

Gas Mower

The final option is gas mowers. They are popular, easy to use, and really the only option if you have to take care of a really big piece of ground. More expensive models come with bells and whistles like self-propulsion and electric start, but even low-end ones tend to start and work pretty well most of the time. As with electric mowers, you have mulching and bagging options.

The big downside of gas mowers is that they are air-pollution factories. The EPA says lawn mower engines are responsible for five percent of the annual U.S. air pollution. The Union of Concerned Scientists says that using a typical gas-powered lawn mower for one hour puts as much pollution in the air as eight late-model cars all driving for an hour at highway speeds.

In heavily polluted areas, gas lawn mowing is banned on bad air quality days because it contributes so much to ground-level ozone. There are cleaner versions coming onto the market, but they're expensive right now and probably more than you need for your lawn at the moment.

Other considerations with gas mowers are that you have to have a gas can and buy gas for them, and like all engines, they require some maintenance to last and start and run reliably over time.

MOWING WITHOUT A MOWER

The problem with all mowers is that they're big and take a fair amount of space to store. And if your yard is small, there may be a better option.

STRING TRIMMERS

String or line trimmers are those hand-held weed whackers people use to clean up the edges of their lawns. There's a reel of heavy plastic cord that feeds out as it's needed, and the spinning plastic string makes for an effective weed cutter. So why not use one to cut your lawn?

The obvious answer is that they cut a narrow swath, so it will go more slowly than any kind of mower. But if your yard is small—a little 10-by-10 patch of grass in front or back, or even something double that size—a string trimmer really can do the job. They take up next to no room to store, something no mower can say, and are cheaper than the cheapest mower.

It's what we use. Our yard has grass in a 20-by-20 area, and all I need is a little cheap electric string trimmer to keep it neat.

MOWING THE LAWN

Not a whole lot needs to be said here. People argue about the best way to mow a lawn—round and round in decreasing circles, back and forth in straight lines, diagonally, whatever. The truth is people like to argue. Any of it works.

1 . Start by setting the height of your mower. You only have to do this once. Most folks cut their grass too short; what you want is grass about three to three-and-a-half inches tall. You adjust the cutting height by raising or lowering the wheels on your mower. (Do it with the engine off and blades not spinning. Getting your fingers or toes under the spinning blades of a lawn mower is a very, very painful mistake.)

2 . When you start mowing, mow around the edge of your lawn first, and mow around any trees, obstacles, sprinkler heads, or other obstructions you need to avoid. (And seriously try to avoid mowing over raised sprinkler heads. Fountains are nice in Venice, but you don't need one in your front yard.)

3 . Once you've mowed around the edges and obstacles, have at the rest in whatever pattern makes sense to you. If you have a bagging machine, you'll know it's time to empty the bag when you start seeing little grass clumps behind the mower. If your city or county collects green waste, great. If not, see if there is a service in your area that will collect the waste and turn it into compost. There's really no reason grass should end up in a landfill.

HIRING IT OUT
THE LAWNMOWER MAN

If by chance you are responsible for yard care where you live and don't have the time, tools, or interest in doing it yourself, you can hire a lawn service to do it for you. If you can afford it, it's a convenient way to have a nice-looking yard. You can find a service in the local phone book, on Angie's List, or just by talking to the crew that shows up in the neighborhood to take care of someone else's lawn. (Yard guys like being able to do multiple jobs on the same street. It's efficient and profitable.)

Bartering may also be an option. Is there something you can do for a yard-work-loving neighbor? Help them with grocery shopping, pick up their kids from school certain days of the week, or just provide beer and barbecue on a semi-regular basis? Sometimes you just have to make the offer, and they'll do a quick mow for you because they're nice. This works especially well with guys who have those riding lawn mowers, who often need to justify their purchase to themselves (and their spouses!). Just be sure to return the favor later if you can.

WATERING

A NICE REFRESHING DRINK

The other thing you have to do to keep a lawn alive and looking nice is to water it. If your place has built-in sprinklers, and they work, you're ahead of the game. If not, $5 sprinklers attached to a hose work just fine.

HOW MUCH AND HOW OFTEN

Hose and sprinkler

Most folks over-water. Your lawn doesn't need to get watered every day, and depending on how hot it is where you live, may not need it every other day. Two to three times a week is plenty in most climates, for a half-hour to an hour. (One way to tell if your lawn needs watering is to walk across it. If the grass bounces back up in your footprints, it's fine. If it doesn't, it needs a drink.)

What you don't want to do is water a little every day. A little water every day promotes shallow roots and crabgrass. A nice deep watering twice a week promotes deep roots and a healthy lawn.

WHEN TO WATER

It's best to water in the morning, before the heat of the day and when the grass is still wet with dew. It's dumb to water during the hot part of the day because so much of the water you're trying to put on the lawn simply evaporates. Evening is okay, but lawn-care experts say watering at night can promote diseases in your lawn because it stays wet longer. If you've got programmable sprinklers, set them for early morning—6 a.m. or so. If you're doing it with a hose and sprinklers, nobody's gonna ask you to get up at 6 a.m. just to turn them on. Turning on the sprinklers while you watch *Entertainment Tonight* in the evening will be just fine.

One thing to do before you start watering is check your area's watering restrictions. Many communities now ban watering during certain hours or on certain days, and while an illegal watering ticket is certainly better than most tickets you can get, it's still a hassle you don't need. Call your local city hall, check their website, or ask at a nearby nursery or garden shop for the rules where you live.

THE JOYS OF AUTOMATIC SPRINKLERS
WATERING IN THE RAIN

Sprinkler timer and remote

Automatic sprinklers are wonderful. Good systems have sprinklers that cover the whole yard (sometimes in several different blocks that water at different times) and come on at set days and times. With an automatic sprinkler system, you can dial in just the watering that you want—say Monday and Friday mornings from 6 a.m. to 6:35 a.m.

Then the time changes. Or the power goes out. Or it rains for three weeks straight and your sprinklers still come on. Then your sprinklers are coming on at 11:15 a.m. when watering is banned, and you look like a Troglodyte.

The lesson here: Even if your place has automatic sprinklers, you'll have to take a look at them once in a while and may have to reprogram or reset the system. For that you'll need to find the control panel. They are usually indoors—in a garage or mudroom or the like—and are simple dial faces or electronic screens a little bigger then your cell phone. The face may be covered by a flip-open plastic cover (and those are usually green).

SETTING THE SYSTEM

To set the system, you basically have to tell it two things: what day and time it is now, and what days and times you want the sprinklers to come on. Each system is a little different, so if the programming instructions aren't obvious, you'll need the little manual that came with the controller. And because you're in a rental, it's probably long gone. Look around on the controller itself and find the brand and model number and search Google for it. Chances are you'll find the instruction book online.

Many systems also let you put them on hold with just the touch of a single button. Do this if it's raining. There's simply nothing more wasteful than having automatic sprinklers come on when it's raining. When the rains pass, a single touch turns the system back on so it'll catch its next scheduled watering.

A few places may have built-in sprinklers but no automatic controls. In these systems, you spin a dial sticking up out of the ground to turn the sprinklers on and off. It's as easy as it sounds, and beats dragging a hose and sprinkler around.

OTHER LAWN CARE TASKS

THE GREEN, GREEN GRASS OF HOME

While there are people who spend dozens of hours a week fussing with their lawns, it's really not necessary. We have lawns because they're easy and convenient. (There's a reason orchids never became a popular landscaping option.) Watering and mowing cover 90 percent of it. About the only other thing you may want to do is fertilize once or twice a year, and pull or kill any major weed infestations if you get them. A mulching mower takes care of most of the fertilizing automatically. Sprinkling your lawn with some kind of "weed and feed" fertilizer twice a year is about all you need to do. Do it in the spring when the grass is just starting to come back from its winter dormancy, and again in the fall before it yellows and shuts down for the winter.

There are applicators that attach to your hose, and you just spray the stuff all over your lawn, or there are little pellets you can sprinkle by hand or with a hand-held broadcast spreader. Whatever you use, keep it on your lawn. Lawn fertilizers and chemicals are a major source of water pollution when they wash off your lawn into a storm drain and then into the local rivers. (The fertilizers encourage algae growth, using up all the oxygen in the water, and other aquatic life gets choked out.) So if you do use a fertilizer or pesticide, make sure it stays on your lawn and don't use one if it's about to rain. If you use a dry product, sweep it off your driveway and sidewalks back onto your lawn. Little actions like these really do help.

PLANTING PRETTY THINGS

GOING TO POT!

When you're in a rental, chances are you're not going to be doing a whole lot of major and expensive landscaping.

What you might end up doing, though, is planting a few flowers or nice plants in pots. You can move them about the place as the seasons dictate, and take them with you when you move. (True story: When my wife and I moved out of our last rental house, I had a whole trip with just her potted plants, which filled the entire floor of the moving van!)

PICKING PLANTS

When you pick plants for your home, shop at local nurseries or garden shops. They'll give you your best shot at finding something suited to your climate and elevation. Don't be afraid to ask the folks who work there, too. They usually know what they're talking about and are happy to help you find something that will work for you.

Also consider buying native plants for your area. A lot of the plants we're all familiar with aren't natives at all, and some are really just invasive weeds. By picking native plants, you're less likely to have disease and pest problems.

Also consider your yard or house when you're picking plants. If it's always sunny, you're stuck with sun-loving plants. (There are usually tags on the plants themselves that tell you if the plant likes full sun, partial sun, partial shade, or full shade.) If you're in the mountains surrounded by big trees and never get much sun, you'll need to choose shade-lovers. Some like a lot of light. Some don't. Put the plant in the kind of light it likes or it'll just die.

POTTING YOUR PRETTY PLANTS

The plants you buy in a nursery will usually be planted in small flats or one-gallon plastic pots. Chances are, since you're buying a plant to make your house look nice, you'll want a nicer-looking pot. Choose one slightly bigger than the pot the plant is in now. (If you have small flowers in six-packs, you can put several into a larger pot.) Clay pots hold moisture better than plastic, but are a lot heavier. The one absolutely critical feature for any pot is that is has to have a hole in the bottom for water to drain out. If there's no hole, it'll kill your plant. (It is possible to drill a hole in a clay pot—even a glazed one—with a masonry bit in your drill, but you're better off finding a pot with a hole in it already.)

DRAINAGE

Drainage is important. If water just sits in your pot and stagnates, your plant will die. Some gardeners put a layer of broken pot bits in the bottom of a new pot. (If you have any number of plants at all, you will have broken pot bits. If you're just starting out, ask the garden center for a few broken pieces.) You can use gravel in the very bottom, too.

TRANSPLANTING

Transplanting is a matter of taking the plant from the plastic nursery pot and moving it into the new pot. Get some potting soil—it's cheap—and put a few inches in the bottom of your new pot over the broken pot bits. Take the plant in both hands and turn it upside down, pulling the old plastic pot away. Now take a look at the roots.

If there's lots of dirt around the edges, you're ready to re-plant. Slip the plant into the new pot and fill in around it with potting soil. You don't want to pack it in there tight, but you do want all the gaps filled. Press the soil into the pot gently with your fingers or a stick and when it's all full and the plant is stable, give it a little water.

ROOT BOUND PLANTS

Some plants are root bound—their roots have gotten too big for the pot they were in and when you pull them out of the plastic nursery pot pretty much all you can see are roots tightly wound around the edges. If that's the case with your plant, you have a bit more work to do before repotting it.

1 . First, you need to loosen the roots. Plants draw in water and nutrients through tiny hairs at the end of their small roots, and if the plant's roots are all pressed in on themselves, those root hairs aren't reaching the soil. So carefully pull the roots apart. Bonsai growers use a chopstick or a small hook, but any nearby stick will do.

2 . Second, take a look at the pot you're about to put the plant into. If the pot is about the same size as the pot it came out of, you're asking for trouble. It'll just get root bound again. You can either put it in a bigger pot, or trim the roots back. (You can trim roots by about a third without killing the plant, but you do need to baby it for the first week or two if you do.) The bigger-pot route is better. Some gardeners check to see if the plants they're looking at are root bound before they leave the nursery so they can buy the right-sized pot for them. It's a good idea.

WATERING POTTED PLANTS

More potted plants have been killed by too much water than by not enough. Like your lawn, your plants don't need water every day. Water when the plants just start to look wilty. It'll usually be three or four or five days. (Phoenix is probably an exception.) Pretty soon it'll be second nature.

If you have to leave your plants unattended for several days—spring break, let's say—you have a couple of options. If you have automatic sprinklers you can set them somewhere where the sprinklers will water them. A neighbor might be nice enough to stop in. You can also set your pots in a shallow pan of water, which will keep them moist. Whichever option you choose, make sure to give them a good watering before you go, and hope for the best.

One last thought about potted plants. They make great gifts. If you're moving to a new area or just don't have the room to take your plants with you, shower the neighborhood with give-away plants. They make people happy!

CHAPTER 9:

TOOLS AND HARDWARE STORES

If your eyes glaze over at the mere mention of tools, think of them as new shoes or Gap tees. They're simply useful, necessary items. (Fortunately for the tool companies, there are some of us out there who love tools as much as some folks love shoes, so it all works out.) And if you have a car, a bike, or an apartment, there are a few tools you're going to want to have around. This chapter will tell you what those tools are.

THE BASIC TOOL KIT

TOOLS YOU REALLY NEED

These are the essentials. You can get them all for less than the price of a giant pizza, and when your cute new neighbor moving in across the hall asks if you have a hammer, it'll be worth every penny. So don't delay!

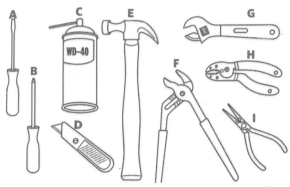

(A) Flat-head screwdriver (B) Phillips-head screwdriver (C) WD-40
(D) Box cutter (E) Hammer (F) Channel-lock pliers (G) Adjustable
wrench (H) Pliers (I) Needle-nosed pliers

A HAMMER

Just your basic household hammer, with a pounding side on one end (the face) and a curved claw behind it. Use the pounding side to tap nails into your walls, and the claw to pry them back out.

A couple of semi-boring safety tips about hammers: One, try not to hammer your thumb. When you're holding a nail, tap it lightly at first until it holds itself, then move your hand safely out of the way before you hit it harder. (If all you're doing is setting it into a wall to hang a picture from, it won't be necessary to hit it harder.)

If you're actually using nails to hold two pieces of wood together and do need to hit the nails harder, safety glasses are a good idea. Every now and then when you're hammering you'll hit the edge of the nail, and it'll zing out and fly around the room. Safety glasses will keep it from zinging into your eye. If you can't bring yourself to wear shop-dork safety glasses, at least wear regular eyeglasses or even lightly tinted sunglasses. Personally I've always felt a few moments of looking dorky in safety glasses was better than a few hours in an emergency room while some guy tries to pull a chunk of metal out of my eyeball.

SCREWDRIVERS

Butter knives do not count! You need real screwdrivers, and

you need at least two—a standard, flat-bladed screwdriver and a Phillips head screwdriver. The tip of the Phillips comes to a point and looks like a +. The screws have the same crossed pattern. If you have to buy screws for some reason, it's easier to drive Phillips screws than standard ones. The cross shape of Phillips screws has more surface area for the screwdriver to hold onto, so it slips less and works better.

They make Phillips and standard screwdrivers in a variety of sizes and lengths. Start with medium-sized screw-drivers—they'll be about nine inches long—and buy or borrow bigger or smaller ones later if you need them.

ADJUSTABLE WRENCH

Technically this is called an "open-end adjustable wrench," but most people call it a crescent wrench. (It does not, however, look like a crescent. It got it name because it was made popular by the Crescent Tool Company.)

This wrench has a handle, and the business end adjusts to fit around different sized nuts and bolts. To adjust it, you just have to spin a little gear with your thumb. The beauty of an adjustable wrench is that it can take the place of a whole slew of single-sized wrenches, and it doesn't care whether the nuts and bolts you're dealing with are SAE (American sized, or fractions) or metric. You just dial up the size you need, and you're good to go.

Buy two of these.

Yep, buy two. One small and one medium. Let's say you need to adjust the seat on your bike and need to loosen the nut. If you only have one wrench, you'll put it over the nut, turn it, and the nut and bolt will both turn as one. To get the nut off, you also need to hold the bolt still, and that's where the second wrench comes in.

One more thought. They've recently come out with an automatic adjustable wrench. It's battery powered, and when you press a button, the jaws automatically squeeze in to accommodate whatever sized nut or bolt you're dealing with. I'm not going to say this is the dumbest idea in the last quarter-century, but it may be in the running. It doesn't make the wrenching part of the job any easier, it just saves you from spinning a little wheel with your thumb. (It can also break or need a new battery.) Toolmakers come out with "improvements" like this all the time so they can keep selling tools. Their problem is that a well-made tool, especially a hand tool like a wrench, will essentially last forever. I have crescent wrenches my grandfather used in the 1930s, and they're just as good today as they were then. So they try to make them obsolete so people will buy new stuff.

Stick to basic hand tools without extra gee-gaws and bells and whistles and you'll be fine.

PLIERS

I'm hesitant to put pliers on this list, because pliers are the most-abused tool in most homes. They're used for jobs they were never intended for and make those jobs harder—if not impossible.

Pliers are holders, not turners. Use pliers for holding things too small, too hot, or too sharp to handle with your fingers. Use wrenches to turn nuts and bolts. The problem with pliers is they get used as wrenches—and they make lousy wrenches—and you end up rounding off the points of the nut or bolt you're trying to deal with. (Then it's really a problem because now even a wrench won't turn it.)

Get a pair of pliers—but please only use them for pinching or holding or bending stuff. They come in all shapes and sizes (I just counted and have 19 various kinds and sizes of pliers) but start with a medium-sized pair that adjusts and fits in your hand. Needle-nosed pliers, which have long beak-like jaws, are very handy for holding small stuff or reaching into tight places.

A RAZOR KNIFE OR BOX CUTTER

This can be from a stationery store or a hardware store. I've found more uses for a razor knife than I can remember. You will, too. X-Acto is a common brand.

WD-40

WD-40 isn't an all-purpose lubricant. Do not, for instance, spray it into the bearings of your roller blades. (It's way too thin to protect the bearings, and if you do use it you'll have to buy new bearings in very short order.)

WD-40 is great for sticky locks, squeaky hinges, and keeping stuff from rusting. In fact, the WD-40 stands for "water displacing, 40th attempt," because it was the chemist's fortieth try at developing a good rust preventer.

They sell small cans the size of a roll of quarters that will hold you for a long time.

ANY OTHER TOOL
YOUR POSSESSIONS REQUIRE

Yeah, the category is a bit of cheat. But your basic, essential tool kit really should contain any other tool you need to assemble, maintain or repair your possessions. If your bike has Allen bolts as fasteners, you need the right-sized Allen wrenches to turn those fasteners. If your new put-it-together-yourself desk comes with square-drive screws, you'll need the little square-headed driver that comes with the kit. And you need to save it! Tape it inside a drawer, because it'll come in very handy if you ever have to disassemble the desk to move it, or even tighten up a fastener that's come loose.

A TOOL BOX

No need to get crazy here, but a small plastic tool box to keep all your tools together in one obvious place is a good investment. They come in different colors, if décor is an issue.

THE MEDIUM
TOOL KIT

TOOLS YOU'LL EVENTUALLY NEED

These are tools that you will eventually own—every kitchen junk drawer in America has some of these—so you may as well join the club. (Except you'll keep yours in a nice toolbox.)

TAPE MEASURE

Want to know if that couch on Craig's list will fit along that

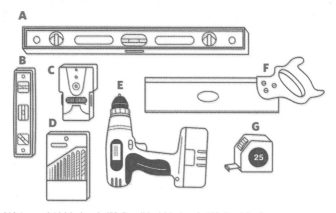

(A) Large bubble level (B) Small bubble level (C) Stud finder
(D) Drill bits (E) Cordless drill (F) Handsaw (G) Tape measure

wall? (Or through your door?) If that new TV will fit in
your entertainment center? How much taller those new
heels make you? You'll need a tape measure.

Buy a basic steel tape measure, 25 feet long, one inch wide.
(Narrower ones are lighter but the tape doesn't hold its
shape as well, so they can be harder to use alone.) It'll be the
last tape measure you'll ever need to buy.

STUD FINDER

We talked about these back in the Apartments chapter
(page 122). They find the 2-by-4 studs holding your walls
up, and if you want to hang anything heavy on your walls,
you're going to need one of these. Some models detect elec-

trical current and metal behind the wall as well—so you can avoid hitting wiring or copper pipes—but even a basic one will find studs. Prices start under $20 and go up.

CORDLESS DRILL/DRIVER
Unlike the automatic crescent wrench, these were a great and handy invention. This should be the first power tool you own. It may be the only one you ever own.

Cordless drills drill holes (naturally) and drive and remove screws. With different attachments, you can use them to sand stuff smooth or polish stuff shiny. Some have built-in batteries and you plug the recharging cord directly into the tool. Others have removable battery packs. They each have advantages. The built-in battery tools tend to be smaller and lighter, but need recharging more frequently. They're fine for occasional household use. The tools with removable batteries are heavier but hold a charge longer. Because they have external rechargers, you can buy an extra battery pack and always have one recharging while you use the other.

Also, batteries range from nine volts to 19.2 or higher. The bigger the number, the more power the tool will have and the longer it will last between recharges. (Also, the more expensive it will be.) A good strategy is to buy a tool one step below the top power tools. If 19.2 volts is the highest power drill you see, look at the 18 volt drills. They'll be steeply discounted and almost as good.

Drill-drivers come with screwdriver bits—both Phillips and standard—but you may need to buy a small pack of drill bits as well. Figure on spending $25 for a cheap and light-duty drill-driver up to $75 or more for a higher-end product. Better yet, if you have an uncle or relative who likes tools, ask for one for Christmas or your birthday. People who like tools like buying tools—even for someone else. And even if they buy a new top-of-the-line drill for themselves and hand down their old one to you, you're still ahead of the game.

A HANDSAW

There are dozens of different kinds of handsaws out there, from tiny pull-cut finish saws to whacking big, rough saws for cutting down trees. You want something small and compact. A handy-sized saw is a backsaw. It's technically used to cut clean angles in wood, but it's a decent size for many household tasks. They're about 18 inches long, and the blade is rectangular. You won't need a saw very often, but every now and then you're going to run into a piece of wood that's sticking out, is just a little too long, or for some other reason needs to be a little shorter. (A new closet bar, for instance.)

When that happens, a saw is the only answer.

BUBBLE LEVEL

To get shelves or pictures straight, you'll need a level. A bubble level is essentially a straight plastic or aluminum bar with clear tubes installed in it. There's liquid and a bubble in each of the tubes, and when the level is perfectly straight, the bubble will sit evenly between two lines. (The old insult "half-a-bubble-off-plumb" comes from this. Plumb means straight upright.) Levels work really well.

Let's say you're installing shelves and want to screw the brackets into two studs 16 inches apart. Screw one bracket in place, then put one end of your level on top of it. Hold the other bracket against the next stud over and set the other end of the level on top of it. Now just move the bracket up or down until the bubble in your level rests dead even between the marks. When it's there, mark the mounting holes for your second bracket, take the level down, and screw in the bracket at your marks. Your shelves will be perfectly straight.

A level that's two feet long will handle most of what you'll ever need to do. I also have a small level, about eight inches, that's handy for checking pictures and mirrors and stuff.

THE ADVANCED TOOL KIT

TOOLS YOU MAY NEVER NEED BUT WILL IMPRESS THE HOTTIE ACROSS THE HALL

These are a few more things worth picking up. Many of them do what your basic tools do but do them better.

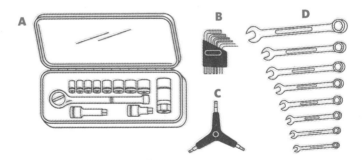

(A) Rachet and socket set (B) Hex wrenches (or Allen wrenches)
(C) Three-in-one hex wrench (D) Combination wrench set

COMBINATION WRENCH SET

Combination wrenches have an open end on one side that looks like a U and a circle on the other (called the box end). They come in both SAE (American or fractional sizes, like 3/8s, 9/16s, etc.) and metric. Best-case scenario, you have both. If you're only going to own one set, pick whatever matches your car. If it's American-made, get SAE. If it's an import, get metric.

Why do you need combination wrenches if you have open-end adjustable wrenches? Because they work better. The adjustable wrenches substitute for lots of different wrench sizes, but they don't hold as cleanly as single-sized wrenches. Adjustable wrenches also can't reach into all the spaces a slimmer combination wrench can. You can get a decent set for under $20 if you shop well.

RATCHET AND SOCKET SET

It's the same principle here. Ratchets are handles. Sockets snap onto ratchets and fit over nuts and bolts. Watch a mechanic at work, and she'll use a combination wrench to hold a bolt still and a ratchet and socket to loosen or tighten the nut. These also come in SAE and metric sizes, but good starter sets often include both. You need a socket set to assemble many bunk bed frames because the bolt heads are recessed into the frame, and a socket is the only way to hold them still. Figure about $20 for a decent starter set on sale.

HEX WRENCH SET

These are also called hex keys or Allen wrenches. (I don't know who Allen was.) They are hexagonal lengths of steel bent in the shape of an L. Rather than fitting around the head of a bolt, they fit into a hex-shaped hole in the bolt. Like everything else, they come in SAE and metric sizes. Many modern bikes use hex-headed fasteners, and if yours does, you'll need hex wrenches, probably metric. A lot of put-it-together furniture usually includes the necessary hex wrench in the package.

SHOPPING FOR TOOLS

SOLD!

Here's the cool thing about hand tools—the good ones last dang near forever. So if you're shopping for the basic hand tools in this chapter, you don't have to buy new tools. Go to a big thrift store or a flea market, and you'll be able to find most everything here, and you'll pay a buck or two per tool. It doesn't get any cheaper than that. Before you buy a used level, check it. Line it up on the wall so the bubble shows level and make pencil marks at both ends. Now flip it over like a propeller and check your marks. If the bubble again shows level, it's working right and worth buying.

If you can't find a decent socket set or the combination wrenches at the thrift store, any Sears or major auto chain store will have them. Lowes also has a good selection of reasonably priced hand tools. Watch for sales and you'll save a bunch.

The only tool on the list above I'd really try to buy new is the cordless drill. The batteries that come with them all eventually stop holding a charge, and that's probably why its former owner got rid of it. Save on everything else but buy a new drill.

HARDWARE STORES

NEW PLACES TO SHOP

When it comes to hardware stores, you've got choices. There are the huge home improvement chains like Home Depot and Lowes, medium-sized regional chains like Orchard Supply Hardware in California, and small local hardware stores often affiliated with Ace or True Value.

The big ones stock more stuff and often have better prices, but even contractors get lost inside them and finding someone to help you is a sketchy proposition. The medium ones have better service and a decent selection of stuff. But when you're just getting started in this whole repair and maintenance thing, the small local stores are the way to go. What's most valuable right now is an employee who can help you find the doodad you need, or tell you what else will work.

In a good hardware store, you should be able to tell the employee what you need to do or show them the broken thing you're trying to fix and they'll not only get you the right stuff, they'll tell you the tricks to using it. (If any place you shop can't do this or makes you feel dumb for asking, shop somewhere else.) The only downside to small local stores is that sometimes they won't have what you need.

BUY THE RIGHT THING THE FIRST TIME

The easiest way to make sure you come back with the right part is to take the problem part with you when you go. Say your bike seat comes loose and you look and notice the nut that's supposed to hold the mounting bolt tight is missing. Take the bolt with you to the store. Or the new computer desk you're putting together is supposed to come with five screws and it comes with four. Take one of those four with you. It's much easier to match an actual part than a memory or a sketch.

Maybe there was a party, and one of your roommate's treasured possessions got broken. Take a piece of it with you to the store. There are lots of kinds of glues out there, and by seeing exactly what it is you're trying to repair the hardware store guy will help you get the right one.

NAILS, SCREWS, AND OTHER DOODADS

In a hardware store, you'll see an aisle for "Hardware." It isn't actually redundant. The word *hardware* refers to nails and screws and staples and dozens of other similar products, and they actually do fill up a whole aisle.

Fortunately, you really only need to buy a few of them at first.

NAILS

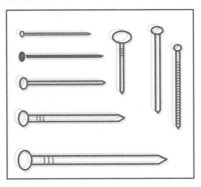

Yep, there are a bunch of different kinds of nails, and the differences are denoted by an arcane naming system that bears no resemblance to reality. (People actually disagree over the origins of the naming system.) Lucky you!

The good thing is that you probably just need nails to hang stuff on the wall, so there's really only two kinds you need to know. One is a finish nail. These are a little over an inch long, and instead of a flattened round head where you hit it with a hammer, they just have a little ball-shaped end slightly bigger then the nail itself. They were designed this way so you can drive them completely under the front edge of the wood you're nailing and cover them with a little putty. Obviously, if you're using them to hang objects on your wall, you won't be driving them that deep!

The other nail to know is what is called a six-penny box nail. You'll see it noted on the box as 6d. These are two inches long and do have flattened heads for hitting with the hammer. They're strong enough to hold anything you ought to be using a nail to hold anyway, and if it's really heavy (more than 20 pounds) you should use a screw instead of a nail.

In case you care, the arcane naming system is the penny system. In the United States, nails aren't one-inch nails, two-inch nails, etc.; they're four-penny, five-penny, and six-penny nails. Blame the British. People still disagree if the system evolved from the weight of the nails, because the British did use the pennyweight system of weights for a while, or if it referred to how many pennies it cost you for 100 nails. (The smaller the penny number, the smaller then nail.)

Here's where it really gets screwy. Canada, which didn't have a revolution to throw off the British Crown, describes nails in inches. A 6d nail here is a two-inch nail there. Go figure. The rest of the world, naturally, uses the metric system and lists nails by their length in millimeters.

SCREWS

As many kinds of nails as there are, there are even more screws. Screws do the same job as nails—hold two things together—but do it better. Nails back out or twist out under pressure. Screws don't. Screws do take longer to use, and do require drilling pilot holes in many cases. They're also more expensive, so they'll never completely replace nails.

For general hanging stuff on the wall or holding this edge of an old dresser to that edge of an old dresser, here's what to get: $1^5/8$ or 2-inch-long "coarse-thread drywall screws." The hardware store gal will call them Sheetrock screws. (Sheetrock is a brand of drywall—the stuff that forms most modern walls.) These are great general-purpose screws with wide threads that hold really well. Buy a one-pound box.

There are literally hundreds of thousands of other things in hardware stores, and some of them you may eventually need to buy. They do sell shoes and T-shirts there if nothing else!

INDEX